JEREMY TAYLOR AND THE GREAT REBELLION

His polemical works you may skip alto-
gether, unleess you have a taste for the
exertions of vigorous reason and subtle distinguishing on interesting topics
—CHARLES LAMB

Jeremy Taylor and the Great Rebellion

A Study of His Mind and Temper in Controversy

FRANK LIVINGSTONE HUNTLEY

Ann Arbor
THE UNIVERSITY OF MICHIGAN PRESS

For
John, Janet, Sylvia, Christopher, and James

Preface

This book on Jeremy Taylor does not touch on his best known devotional works, *Holy Living* and *Holy Dying*, nor his theologically most important ones, the sermons and "cases of conscience." There already exist studies of his piety, homiletics, and casuistry, as well as of his style. Rather, this book attempts to introduce the literary student, first, to Taylor's mind in controversy, and, second, to the way he conducted his arguments in an age unparalleled in history for the violence of its religious disputation. Browne's irenic *Religio Medici* was composed by a mind purposely withdrawn from the drums and tramplings of the Civil War. And many have seen fit to think of Taylor during the same war only as a secluded spiritual adviser to a nobleman's family at Golden Grove. But Jeremy Taylor, a marked Laudian figure to the Presbyterian political leaders and a chaplain loyal to a falling king, was caught up intellectually, morally, politically, and even physically in the Great Rebellion at the very time when his powers as a writer were at their height.

Students of literature are, or should be, more concerned with wholes than with excerpts of beautiful prose. Taylor's arguments are wholes, and an important plea like *The Liberty of Prophesying*, for example, has never been analyzed as a single piece of persuasion in the most divisive period of England's history. Neither a précis nor an analysis, of course, is a substitute for reading the argument itself. The difference between a précis and an analysis is that the analysis leaves the conclusions and points where the author put them rather than lifting them from their formal setting for comment. We have admirable summaries of Taylor's controversial views by Tulloch, Jordan, Bolton, and Trevor-Roper; this book, I believe, is the first analysis—which, like an explication of a poem, discerns the organic relationship of parts to the whole which a swift reader often misses and which can be constantly checked against the text. The poet or orator selects and arranges his parts as means to an end; the critic must perceive their unity and the principles of their ordering. Much older than "the new criticism," the procedure has always sought to bring together the speaker, the speech itself, and the occasion and audience which demanded it.

Perhaps Taylor's stature in literature or ecclesiastical history scarcely deserves so specialized a treatment. Yet the study of any aspect of his life and work that can shed light on the mind that fashioned the English prose by which he chiefly lives is justified. Controversy, that enlisted the mind and energy of another man gifted in language during the same Civil War, John Milton, is an important key to the mind and the temper of his poetry.

Finally, since Taylor has always been admired for his piety and beautiful bits of prose but was condemned in the nineteenth century by Heber, his biographer, and by Coleridge, his critic, for his controversial writings, such a study as this seems timely. From the more ecumenical perspective of the twentieth century and with the advances that have been made in our knowledge of seventeenth-century rhetorical skills, we can reexamine this central part of his life and thought. While I try to give both sides of each controversy, Taylor's position is bound to emerge the more clearly as the book is designed to hear him speak.

I am grateful for the kind wisdom of two former teachers: Charles Wager, at Oberlin, who introduced me to the beauties

Preface

of the literature of the Via Media; and Ronald S. Crane, at Chicago, who made me love to analyze argument. With some trepidation I submitted this work to two theologically trained friends and neighbors: one, a Presbyterian, the Reverend Ernest Campbell, now minister at Riverside Church in New York, who read my chapter on original sin; and the other, the Reverend Gordon M. Jones, Jr., Anglican, who, after reading the whole, went over with me every theological crux. Even his acumen and charity, however, cannot excuse any errors which may still lurk in my interpretations.

Especially am I grateful to Austin Warren, whose feeling for and knowledge of seventeenth-century modes of thought and present-day good English have made this book much better than had his rigorous but soft pencil not gone up and down the margins of its manuscript.

For enabling me to follow the footsteps of Jeremy Taylor through England, Wales, and Ireland, I thank the University of Michigan Horace H. Rackham School of Graduate Studies.

Most of all I am thankful to Katharine for enduring the groans and ecstasies of a husband's "profession of English," and for presiding over the early affairs of the persons to whom this book is dedicated.

Ann Arbor, Michigan

Contents

Taylor's Polemic Genius and His Three Wartime Controversies

I

Matthew Arnold, from a knowledge of Taylor perhaps gained from an anthology of his "gems," helped to promote the opposition between the kind of prose Taylor wrote and good thinking. In "The Literary Influence of the Academies" (1865) he said that England has the energy and the genius to produce the poetry of a Shakespeare but no such power as that of France in prose. Hence Newman is right, Arnold continues, in using the word "note" in describing certain English prose as having "the note of sanctity" or "the note of antiquity." Of Taylor, then, Arnold concludes that he (with Burke) has "the note of provinciality." He quotes "So have I seen a river" from Lady Carbery's funeral sermon, and sets beside it the intellectual power of Bossuet. Burke and Taylor are "at too great a distance from the centre of good taste"; both are rich, imaginative, but provincial. In their prose, Arnold says, they seldom reach that high level of intelligence called "classical."[1]

The charge of unintellectuality was made more serious by Sir James Stephens in *Horae Sabbaticae* (1892). He asserted that Taylor "was unaware of the importance of having single and distinct meanings for fundamental terms, and the consequence is, that he used them in a great variety of senses, meaning by the same word the most different things at different times."[2] Yet this is actually no more than thinkers have been doing from Plato, through Dryden, to T. S. Eliot. Anyone persuading us to the truth of his view of love, or justice, or (in the case of Dryden) that a good play should be not only "just" but also "lively" must give us a dozen meanings to the terms, which, by epiphanic increments, gradually attain their fullness as we proceed. In essays of this type, and they are both more numerous and more "literary" than the other, one can no more insist on terminological stasis than he can stop the character of Hamlet. As Hamlet's character develops from the beginning to the end of the play, so does Sir Philip Sidney's term "right poetry." To use terms in this way is not to be unintellectual. It is rather a sign that one's forebears are not Aristotle and Aquinas, but Plato, Clement, Montaigne, and St. Paul.

Taylor was not a systematic theologian or philosopher, but a Christian humanist—"hugely versed in all the polite parts of learning," his friend Bishop Rust said; Taylor "had thoroughly concocted all the ancient moralists, Greek and Roman, poets and orators; and was not unacquainted with the refined wits of the later ages, whether French or Italian." As an Anglican apologist, Taylor was a rhetorician who, driven by necessity into controversy, expended every linguistic talent he possessed to win men to particular attitudes of mind, modes of thinking, and courses of action during a Civil War.

Controversy is the anvil on which certain kinds of truth must be hammered out, and the seventeenth century argued, controverted, defended, attacked, animadverted, and animadverted on animadversions on every conceivable topic—religion, science, politics, morality, economics, persecution, the theater, emigration, love. But during the Civil War, in which Taylor argued for the losing side, the major issues were religious and constitutional, or more specifically, questions of inner and outer authority. In those days the position one took meant freedom, personal safety, imprisonment, mutilation, or death.

That Taylor was well prepared to defend the Anglican and Royalist cause is shown by the bibliography he prepared in response to a plea (on January 13, 1660) "to design a short and useful catalogue of practical divinity books" for Trinity College, Dublin. The bibliography contains mostly controversy, for, as he wrote, "Hee that would improve in the understanding of the doctrine of the church of England, so as to be able to teach others, must bee careful to understand, and bee very perfect to every part of it" (I, lxxxix).[3] And, "For the understanding and abilities to proove and defend . . . [the church of England's doctrines], you must acquaint yourselfe with the positive and polemic discourses of such as are most eminent amongst us." He then compiles a list of books in three categories: liturgy, discipline, and doctrine. In the first, he recommends Edward Fisher's argument for Anglican festivals, and his own *Episcopacy Asserted*. In the next category, polity, he insists on Henry Hammond's *Dissertationes Quatuor* of 1650 *contra* Blondel, and his own argument for bishops over presbyters. He especially commends the late king's controversy with the Scottish Presbyterian Alexander Henderson, published in 1649, on the episcopal insistence on *The Book of Common Prayer*. The final category, doctrine, is the largest and most stormy. Its first item is the controversy between Archbishop Laud and the Jesuit "John Fisher," which took place on May 24, 1622, and was published by royal command.[4] For the doctrine of the Holy Eucharist, Taylor recommends his own argument in *The Real Presence* and Bishop John Overal's defense of the Anglican view. Among many others, Taylor finally recommends Richard Montague, the famous author of *Appello Caesarem* (1625), who in his own words to Cosin stood "in the gap against puritanism and popery, the Scylla and Charybdis of Ancient Piety."[5] Drawing up three propositions, this Anglican divine promised to join the Roman Catholic church as soon as any Roman Catholic could prove them to be untrue. He was challenged in Matthew Kellison's *A Gag for the New Gospel*. The bishop (he became bishop of Chichester) replied immediately in a book entitled *A Gagg for the New Gospell? No. A New Gagg for the Old Goose* (1624). Gardiner calls this work "a temperate exposition of the reasons which were leading an increasing body of scholars to reject the doctrines of Rome and of Geneva alike."[6]

"In the reading these authors I have recommended to you," Taylor continues, "pray observe what quotations they have, that thereby you may perceive what authors they make use of and especially read; for 'tis likely they are the best books" (I, xc). Like most scholars, then, Taylor read footnotes too.

In any argument one must start somewhere; he must have grounds or areas of agreement on which to erect a persuasive for those things to be proved. Grounds are axioms; they are unarguable because they are shared matters of belief. In temperament Taylor was religious, rational, and practical; and the major grounds for all his arguments are a belief in God, a trust in right reason, and an assumption that no system is worth anything unless it works. His belief in God he shared with all Christians, and "right reason" appealed to those unaffected by bitterness and passion. But his ground of practicality was shared by almost everyone, and is so pervasive in his writings that it demands further definition.[7]

Taylor called it "economy," a term employed two hundred years later by Newman. "We shall find Christianity to be the easiest and the hardest thing in the world," Taylor said to a congregation at the University of Dublin; "it is like a secret in arithmetic, infinitely hard till it be found out by a right operation, and then it is so plain, we wonder we did not understand it earlier" (VIII, 364). Taylor always begins where his audience is; like an expert teacher he reaches their minds first by touching on what they know, and then, raising them step by step, ends in a clear demonstration which they would earlier have thought impossible to grasp. In another sermon Taylor stresses "the economy of this divine philosophy" (VIII, 375), and throughout his career "God's economy" is perhaps his favorite phrase. The meaning of the term the *Oxford English Dictionary* furnishes is: "The method of divine government of the world, or of a specific department or portion of that government," and the *OED*'s citation of the first use is Jeremy Taylor's *The*

4

Worthy Communicant (1660): "All this is the method and economy of heaven." The word comes from *oikos* ("house") and *nomos* ("management"), and hence is joined to the meaning of stewardship. It is a practical, humble, and homely word, part of the great body of commercial metaphor in Christian thought. For example, though every sin provokes divine anger, Taylor knew that there is mercy "by the economy of God and the divine dispensation" (VII, 139). He believed that God so rules His creation that He achieves His ends, which are always great, through the smallest amount of means, costly though those means sometimes seem to us. Economy is not reduction of expense; it is a ratio between means and ends.

Controversy itself is uneconomical where the expenditures of a man's genius are worth more than the goals which they buy, and Taylor entered into controversy only when he was convinced the goal was worth fighting for. "Skill in controversies," he confessed,

> . . . [is] the worst part of learning, and time is the worst spent in them, and men the least benefited by them; that is, when the questions are curious and impertinent, intricate and unexplicable, not to make men better, but to make a sect. But when the propositions disputed are the foundation of faith, or lead to good life, or naturally do good to single persons or public societies, then they are part of the *depositum* of Christianity, of the "analogy of faith" [cf. Rom., 12:6], and for this we are by the apostle commanded to "contend earnestly"; and therefore controversies may become necessary . . . (VI, 173).

"Though accomplished even beyond his contemporaries," wrote the Reverend R. Cattermole in 1834, "in an age abounding in learned theologians in the use of every weapon of polemical warfare, the mind of Jeremy Taylor was not formed for controversy; and when he entered in it, it was never for the triumph of an opinion, but for the extension of truth and the promotion of godliness."[8]

The three controversies he entered into during the Civil War he believed to be worth contending for earnestly because their very disputation was an economical means to the greater end of advancing real religion. "My purpose is not to dispute," he said, "but to persuade, not to confute anyone but to instruct those that need; not to make a noise, but to excite devotion; not to enter into curious but material enquiries . . ." (VIII, 9). To the lessons in grammar, rhetoric, and logic that he had learned in school and university, he now added a passionate urgency. At one point he confesses: "I could possibly say something to satisfy the boys and young men at a public disputation, but not to satisfy myself, when I am upon my knees and giving an account to God of all my secret and hearty persuasions" (V, 564).

So Taylor's famous similes are but one part of his genius; they come in his sermons and devotions, and very few "gems" appear in the polemical prose that is the subject of this study. Taylor believed, with some of his sectarian brothers' contentious sermons ringing in his ears, that controversies are no more suitable in the pulpit than florid oratory is suitable for winning an argument. When preaching, "Do not trouble your people with controversies," he warns in *The Minister's Duty:*

> A controversy is a stone in the mouth of the hearer, who should be fed with bread, and it is a temptation to the preacher, it is a state of temptation; it engages one side in lying, and both in uncertainty and uncharitableness; and after all, it is not food for souls; it is the food of contention, it is a spiritual law-suit, and it can never be ended; every man is right and every man is wrong in these things, and no man can tell who is right and who is wrong. For as long as a word can be spoken against a word, and a thing be opposite to a thing; as long as places are hard, and men are ignorant or "knowing in part"; as long as there is money and pride in the world, and for ever till men willingly confess themselves to be fools and deceived, so long will the saw of contention be drawn from side to side (VIII, 531–32).

In his University of Dublin sermon, however, he said:

> He therefore who so understands the words of God that he not only believes but loves the proposition; he who

consents with all his heart, and being convinced of the truth does also apprehend the necessity, and obeys the precept, and delights in the discovery, and lays his hand upon his heart, and reduces the notices of things to the practice of duty; he who dares trust his proposition, and drives it on to the utmost issue . . . this man walks in the Spirit . . . (VIII, 378).

Taylor did not withdraw from the Civil War even into the meditative piety of Golden Grove, but like Milton, threw himself into the religious and political turmoils of his day and "drove his propositions on to the utmost issue."

In chronological order Taylor's three Civil War controversies are, first, the arguments for the church and king which he loved and served; second, his classical plea for religious toleration, *The Liberty of Prophesying;* and finally, the longest and most vehemently fought, his controversy on the subject of original sin. The first argument, that for church and king, could be greatly expanded were we to include his dissuasives against the Roman Catholic church, but it has seemed best to exclude them from this study. For one reason, they do not strictly belong to Taylor's Civil War period but were mainly brought on after he became an Anglican bishop in Ireland. For another reason, since his ecumenicity, naturally, did not go as far as ours, it is his anti-Roman pamphlets which today are dated and which perhaps deserve Arnold's epithet "provincial." And yet Bishop Heber called the *Dissuasive from Popery* his most eloquent polemic and his argument against transubstantiation "one of the fullest and ablest expositions of the errors of Popery" (I, ccix). On the other hand, the early arguments for the set forms of Anglican worship are still viable in our day, which has seen a consciousness of form and order even among what used to be the most "enthusiastic" of Protestant sects. His second disputation, for religious toleration, is even more viable. And his final argument before 1660, against reprobationism, anticipates the certain decline of hell and damnation in most present-day Christian thinking. Biographically and historically, then, Taylor's three Civil War controversies come in that particular order: for the Anglican church, 1642–46; for liberty in Biblical interpretation, 1647; and against the Calvinistic interpretation of original sin, 1655–58.

But a not so strict chronology goes deeper than that. The subject of the final argument, the conditions of true repentance, was longest with him; ecclesiastical policy and liturgy, argued first, actually came into his Christian life last. The three controversies also fall into an obverse order according to the age of the issues which brought them about. The first issue, that of the Anglican church, we might say, began with Henry VIII and Archbishop Cranmer; the second issue, on reading the Bible, began with Luther and before him with the church fathers; but the final issue, original sin, referred back to Adam. Taylor's initial argument was of immediate concern, given the parlous state of Anglicans and the king in 1642; his next argument had to do with the spread of Protestantism; and his last controversy sprang from St. Augustine's treatment of the Pelagians. If we may be allowed to think chronologically about the Trinity, Taylor's first argument on the church bespeaks the "final" emanation, God the Holy Spirit; his second argument depends upon the sweet reasonableness of God the Son; and his last is fought for the honor of God the Father.

Aside from chronology, the three controversies fall into an order of decreasing external necessity and consequently, on Taylor's part, of increasing freedom of choice. His earliest arguments for the establishment are a clear call of duty, almost as though they were command performances. To attempt to stem the rebellion against king and bishop, someone had to speak out, preferably one with Jeremy Taylor's gift for polemic: that was in 1642. By 1647, a plea for liberty in the interpretation of Biblical texts is clearly less called for, and that he wrote it when he did is still somewhat of a surprise. But in 1655, who but his own conscience told him to enter a controversy on original sin which he knew would bring down on his head the denunciations of almost all of Christendom including some bishops of his own church?

8

Thus the grounds for each controversy and the methods Taylor employed in argumentation slightly shift as he met each one. For the Anglican church he emphasized the workability of its polity and service. In *The Liberty* he applied *recta ratio* to both Bible and history. In the last controversy he appealed mainly to the glory of God and the best means to a holy life. His ends throughout are always three—civil, ethical, and religious; or, the just demands of government, moral behavior, and piety. But they are given an emphasis by their increasing importance. In 1642 it proved futile to argue for the divine right of the government of Charles the First; in 1647, even his rational proofs that toleration is the better way did not end the ecclesiastical and political bickering; in 1655, he boldly took it upon himself to show that repentance for actual, not imputed, sin is the one thing necessary. The first is "asserted"; the second, argued; in the last, he pleads. For each argument, also, his friends and protectors diminish in prestige, leaving Taylor, as it were, standing more and more alone: from the king and archbishop, to two noblemen, Sir Christopher Hatton and the Marquis of Carbery, and finally, to a plain citizen, John Evelyn, diarist and virtuoso.

Most significantly Taylor's three Civil War controversies fall into a pattern of widening concern and a true hierarchy of value. And yet Bishop Heber, in his account of Taylor's polemical writings, gives them a decreasing amount of space: sixteen pages for the Anglican church, twelve pages for religious toleration, and only ten pages of pious regret for Taylor's longest and climactic argument on original sin. Taylor was moving from the outside to the inside: from a form of government to man's conscience; from the body of the establishment, through the mind, and finally to the soul. First he spoke for his own party, then for all Protestants, and finally for Christianity. He passed from cult, through creed, into theology, In the seventeenth-century intellectual setting he began with "custom," or the ecclesiastical behavior of a people; rose to "nature," those laws which custom should follow; and ended with IDEA, or the pattern in the mind of God which is imitated first by nature and then by custom. From the Anglican service, Taylor might have chosen for the ordering of his arguments these petitions: (1) "For bishops and other clergy," (2) "For the whole state of Christ's church," and (3) "For all sorts and conditions of men." He himself was quite conscious of the values he found himself successively arguing for: in his new dedication to Sir Christopher Hatton (V, 4) of the reissue in a single volume of the first two controversies, he is aware that in *The Liberty* he seemed to argue against his earlier use of texts and tradition. So he employed a similitude of a fire—pull down the outer buildings to save the great house, then destroy the house itself, if need be, in order finally to save your loved ones.

At the end of another dedication, this one in 1649, of the second edition of the argument for the liturgy "To His Most Sacred Majesty" on the eve of the king's execution, Taylor signed himself as "a person indifferent whether I live or die, so I may by either serve God, and God's church, and God's vicegerent." In 1642 and 1646 he did serve the king; in 1647, God's church; and in 1655, God Himself. His polemic prose during the Civil War as means to these ends, then, he believed to be patterned after "the economy of heaven," that is, it had to be practical, rational, and holy.

A Royal Chaplaincy and the Argument for Freedom of the Anglican Church

II

Jeremy Taylor was early singled out for approbation by the highest powers of church and state. When he was hardly out of college at Cambridge, his former chamber fellow, Thomas Risden, asked him to take his place three or four times as part-time lecturer in divinity at St. Paul's in London. Taylor's physical beauty, eloquence, and great learning immediately impressed Archbishop Laud, who, seeing in this young man a valuable future apologist for the church he had determined to revitalize, sent him to his own university, Oxford, for a better orientation in these matters than could be had at Cambridge. On January 14, 1636, Taylor was made fellow at All Souls, Oxford, by Laud himself rather than by the usual way of free election. Shortly after Laud had made him his own chaplain, the archbishop got him appointed "chaplain in ordinary" to His Majesty Charles the First. In this position Taylor probably followed the royal retinue to Oxford at the beginning of the war. By royal mandate he was admitted to the degree of Doctor of Divinity at Oxford.

Surrounded by his military and religious loyalists in the walled town of Oxford, Charles must have felt fairly confident of victory; but the lines of faction had been drawn on the great issue of "authority," both political and religious. In politics the issue was Parliament versus King, though many an Anglican was sympathetic with the rising tide of representative government while many a "Puritan" was royalist. As for matters ecclesiastical, the two factions had been split even in Elizabeth's reign. The Anglicans found their inner religious authority in a reformed and Biblical Protestantism, and yet were jealous of the great Catholic tradition; the Puritans wished to get rid of every vestige of the Roman church. In the external government of religious matters, the Anglicans claimed their king and bishops; the other side elected "lay elders" for themselves. England was assaulted with thousands of books and pamphlets arguing on one side or the other, so many in fact that even G. K. Fortescue's two-volume catalog of the Thomason Tracts cannot count them all. Every document written by a churchman seemed to beget two or three refutations. Against the sectaries and many a liberal Anglican bishop and rector, the high church Laudian Anglicans had to fight for two things they believed to be absolutely essential to the life of their church: the episcopate and the liturgy.[1]

It is no surprise, therefore, that Taylor's initial controversial writings should be a defense of the kind of church polity in which bishops, not presbyters, are its governors; and of a set form for the worship of the church as the body of Christ, called liturgy, as opposed to the extemporary petitions of private individuals used in public gatherings.

Episcopacy

Published in 1642, Taylor's argument for an ecclesiastical polity of bishops has all the appearances of an official stand.[2] The earthly "head" of the church is the sovereign of England; by calling his opposition the *acephali*, or "headless ones," Taylor is asserting the order of king and bishops against the Presbyterians, Independents, and "sectaries" who would have neither. The whole title is worth quoting: *Of the Sacred Order and Offices of Episcopacy, by Divine Institution, Apostolicall Tradition, & Catholike Practice. Together with their Titles of*

A Royal Chaplaincy and Freedom of the Anglican Church

Honour, Secular Employment, Manner of Election, Delegation of their Power, and Other Appendant Questions, Asserted against the Aerians and Acephali, New and Old. By Ier. Taylor, Late Fellow of All-Soules in Oxon. Published by His Maiesties Command, 1642. The running title at the top of each page is "Episcopacy Asserted." On the title page is a quotation from Rom. 13:1: "The powers that be are ordained by God," and like the only preceding publication from Taylor's pen, the sermon on the Gunpowder Plot (1638), this book was published by Lichfield, the printer to Oxford University, of which Laud was chancellor.

The title gives us Taylor's chosen method of debate: it will be historical, based first on the sayings of Christ, then on the acts of the apostles, and finally on the general practice of the Christian church during the first few centuries of its era—a history which the Anglican shares with the Roman Catholic. That is only half the title. The other half, beginning "Asserted against" is directed against all those who oppose the tradition.

Taylor's first argument, accordingly, like so many of his arguments and those of his contemporaries, breaks into two great halves which at first are opposed and then brought together to form a single whole. It is an argument of means-and-ends, then-and-now, recorded history *and* practical politics, revelation-and-experience, what the "thing" being argued for is *in itself* and what it is *for us* in England in the year 1641. Taylor must establish relationships between government on this earth and government in heaven, between subjects and king, priests and bishops, the secular arrangements in time and the religious essentials that are out of time, all mankind and God.

Such a dichotomous mode of procedure springs from Plato, lends itself to Christian discourse, and particularly characterizes much Protestant thinking. The disjunctive was advanced by Ramus as a neo-Platonic and Renaissance revolt against Aristotelian and medieval logic. But more typical of Taylor is the systasis of two terms which forms what may be called a Platonic-Christian dichotomy. At this point we should define it: (1) there is a division into two universal terms; (2) these two are initially opposed to each other, like "body" versus "soul"; (3) at the outset one term is given a higher value than the other—"soul" *above* "body"; (4) they must be of such a kind as to allow their being joined together in order to produce a third entity which is the highest value of all.

An early source is Plato's *Timaeus* (35a) but it is familiar in Christianity from Christ's division of the Ten Commandments into two, and from St. Paul's Hellenized doctrine. To quote Plato on how God created the universe:

> Out of the indivisible and unchangeable, and also out of that which is divisible and has to do with material bodies, he compounded a third and intermediate kind of essence, partaking of the nature of the same and of the other, and this compound he placed accordingly in a mean between the indivisible, and the divisible and material. He took the three elements of the same, the other, and the essence, and mingled them into one form, compressing by force the reluctant and unsociable nature of the other into the same. . . .[3]

Upon this pattern is built a Platonic, Western, and Christian dialectic, like Plato's "visible-*and*-invisible worlds," or "God-*and*-man." As Emerson pointed out in *English Traits*, "The influence of Plato tinges the British genius. Their minds loved analogy; were cognizant of resemblances, and climbers on the staircase of unity. . . . Britain had many disciples of Plato;— More, Hooker, Bacon, Sidney, Chapman, Milton, Crashaw, Norris, Cudworth, Berkeley, Jeremy Taylor. . . ."[4] The pattern must not be confused with the disjunctive. *Black-or-white* and even *black-and-white* is not a true Platonic-Christian dichotomy because, though two and though opposed, there is no hierarchy which would allow the lower to join the higher in order to form a "third" which is most perfect. The Johannine emphasis on *flesh-and-spirit*, on the other hand, meets all four of the criteria; bearing on the central dogma of Christianity, it intends the Incarnation or perfect meeting of God and man in one Person. Again, taking one of Taylor's favorite stories from the Bible, that of Mary and Martha, and listening to echoes from Walter Hilton's *Scale of Perfection*,[5] St. John of the Cross and St. Theresa, we could join Martha as the *active* life to Mary as the *contemplative* life to form a third which, perhaps like Taylor himself, seeks God amid the turmoil of family, ministerial duties, and a political-ecclesiastical Civil War.

We meet the actual pattern everywhere. The greatest love poetry of the Renaissance deals not merely with the woman's body nor merely with her mind, but, like the best of Donne's, with the meeting of souls and bodies to form the most perfect union. Thus the invisible nodule of the compass centrally affirms that the two lovers are "inter-assuréd of the mind," but the argument is whole by virtue of Donne's promise in the last line also to return to his wife's bed. Donne uses a similar technique in "The Ecstasy." Again, Newman, in defining what should be the product of the ideal university, can set up the "gentleman," on the one hand, and the "Christian," on the other, in order to argue for "the Christian-gentleman" in the end. It is ironic that Matthew Arnold should not have recognized this legitimate mode of thinking in Jeremy Taylor when he himself used it to such effect in arguing for that kind of society which is not merely "Hebraic," not (its opposite) merely "Hellenic," but a society of "Hebraic-Hellenes," combining the intellectual virtues of the French and the moral strength of the English into a people of "consciousness-*and*-conscience."

The Platonic-Christian mode emerges in Taylor's argument from the opening sentence of his dedication to Sir Christopher Hatton, as Charles the First has evidently just withdrawn to Oxford and Taylor finds himself forced by deprivation of *person* to seek security in *spirit:*

> Sir, I am engaged in the defence of a great truth, and I would willingly find a shroud to cover myself from danger and calumny; and although the cause both is and ought to be defended by kings, yet my person must not go thither to sanctuary unless it be to pay my devotion, and I have now no other left for my defence; I am robbed of that

15

which once did bless me, and indeed still does (but in another manner), and I hope will do more; but those distillations of celestial dews are conveyed in channels not pervious to an eye of sense, and now-a-days we seldom look with other, be the object never so alluring (V, 9).[6]

The hierarchical procedure continues in the following two paragraphs. The interest of bishops is linked to the king first for their own security; next, "by the obligations of secular [social?] advantages"; and finally, "the bishops' duty to the king derives itself from a higher fountain" (p. 10). The levels of gain are first, that episcopacy is useful; next, that it is honorable; and last, that it is absolutely necessary. Taylor will begin with the words of Christ Himself, that must come from God, and gradually lead his auditors down to everyday practical matters, thus again illustrating his passion for "the economy of heaven" through testing revelation by experience.

The two great "halves" of his argument are signaled for us (p. 192), where in one short linking paragraph he writes: "We have seen what episcopacy is in itself, now from the same principles let us see what it is to us." The proportion is roughly that of four to one, the first part requiring that much more length to demonstrate. Only by a detailed analysis of what episcopacy is *de ipso* can we truthfully weigh what it can do *pro nobis*.

His first half, therefore, must use Scriptural authority as indeed his Presbyterian opponents did, but augmented by tradition, so that Taylor divides *the-thing-itself* into the divine institution, the apostolical tradition, and the authority and practice of the fathers during the first three hundred years of the Christian church. "First, then, that we may build upon a rock" (p. 16), Taylor says, but aware of his opposition he adds: "I hope the adversaries of episcopacy, that are so punctual to pitch *all* [my italics] upon scripture ground, will be sure to produce clear scripture for so main a part of christianity as is the form of the government of Christ's church." Carefully distinguishing by "reason" the clear verses from the obscure, and the relevant from the irrelevant, Taylor secures for himself in

Latin and Greek texts a "liberty of prophesying" from scholarly exegesis. "The sum of all is this: that Christ did institute apostles, and presbyters or seventy-two disciples" (p. 38)—the inevitable Scriptural argument of the Anglican from Cranmer, through Andrewes, Jewel, and Laud. On this stock beginning of a Biblical distinction between the two kinds of church officers, in number, degree, and function, Taylor brings to bear a saying by Theodoret: "The apostles are the twelve fountains, and the seventy-two are the palms that are nourished by the waters of those fountains; for though Christ also ordained the seventy-two, yet they were inferior to the apostles, and afterwards were their followers and disciples" (p. 39). Later in his polemic career we will find Taylor confessing that Scriptural authority alone is an even draw for the two opposing sides.

Proceeding by chronology, Taylor next "asserts episcopacy" by the apostolic tradition in a study of the Acts of the Apostles, and of the witness of Saints James, Simeon, Timothy, Titus, Mark, Linus, Clement, Polycarpus, and a host of others, to "prove" that episcopacy is an apostolical ordinance (p. 69). This includes how the apostles functioned as bishops in Jerusalem, Antioch, Ephesus, and Crete. As he ended his first section on the sayings of Christ with a quotation from Theodoret, so he ends this part by citing Jerome's assertion that there was a " 'public decree issued out in the apostles' times that in all churches one should be chosen out of the clergy, and set over them; viz., to rule and govern the flock committed to his charge" (p. 81).

Finally, after the time of the apostles it was Catholic practice for the first three hundred years or so to set bishops over presbyters by granting them three peculiar offices never allowed to the lesser degree of ecclesiastical officer: ordination, confirmation, and jurisdiction. Taylor's proof here, of course, relies upon the authority of the early church fathers.

To take note of his scholarship at this point of his argument, it is necessary to digress for a moment. In his 1660 bibliography for building a theological library, already referred to, it is very probable that we possess the titles of many of the works which he himself had found to be most useful in laying the foundation of his own religious knowledge. "Read the fathers of the first 300 years at least," he advises, "they are few, and not very voluminous, and they are the surest guides" (I, xc). Along with them one should use Sethus Calvisius's *Chronologia ex autoritate potissimum Sacrae Scripturae* (1605), Bishop Montagu's popular church history that in 1622 answered Baronius, and Isaac Casaubon's *De rebus sacris et ecclesiasticis exercitationes XVI ad Cardinalis Baronii Prolegomena Annales* (1614) in preparation for reading Baronius's *Annals* themselves. For the study of the Bible, the indispensable work is the "Bibliotheca Criticorum," probably the 1611 *Bibliotheca Biblica. Being a Commentary upon all the books of the Old and New Testament*,[7] "of itself an excellent library." By the publication dates of these works in the 1660 list, most of them had been available to Taylor as a divinity student at Cambridge and later as a fellow at All Souls, Oxford.

To return to his present argument, with his indelible signature in debate couched in the first phrase, Taylor thus ends his point that historically only bishops can ordain:

> The sum is this. If the canons and sanctions apostolical; if the decrees of eight famous councils in christendom . . . ; if the constant successive acts of the famous martyr-bishops of Rome making ordinations; if the testimony of the whole pontifical book; if the dogmatical resolutions of so many fathers . . . ; if the constant voice of christendom declaring ordinations made by presbyters to be null and void in the nature of the thing . . . , then it is evident that the power and order of bishops is greater than the power and order of presbyters . . . (p. 122).

This may be true, but the minute citation of historical precedent is not very convincing to an opposition which has set itself to reject that history. Without pausing, Taylor handles in a similar way the testimony of antiquity for bishops alone being granted the power of confirmation, and summarizes the evidence.

Abruptly and confidently he says, "Thus far I hope we are right," and passes on to the last power accorded to bishops as distinct from the presbytery, that is, jurisdiction. The early church gave bishops jurisdiction over particular causes and persons within the church. Over church property, also, they were given a jurisdiction that never belonged to presbyters. They were given power to make church laws and were set over presbyters by the form of their election. After fifty pages, Taylor remarks, "But these things are too known to need multiplication of instances" (p. 175), as if he had proved his point to the hilt from the practice of the early church. "The sum is this: the question was whether or no, and how far, the bishops had superiority over presbyters in the primitive church" (*ibid.*). The question has been resolved. Just as the Roman Catholic would argue against the Protestant that the church preceded the making of the canonical Bible, so Taylor has brought his historical erudition to bear on the proposition that the diocese preceded the congregation (p. 179). This is what "Episcopacy is in itself," as defined in theory and history, Scripture and authority.

Now he passes to the other half, what episcopacy is *for us*. In the old days the previous kind of argument had won over two anti-episcopal groups known as the Aerians and the Acephali;[8] if today (in 1641) there are any members of the same sects around, the same arguments should triumph. Instead of closing here, however, Taylor shifts his grounds with his sights; he appeals to custom, common sense, manners, all of which are a kind of "nature," and which the commonest man can understand and appreciate.

As early as in his dedication to Hatton, Taylor had linked bishops with kings and kings with vicegerents to God, a well-practiced mode of attaining civil peace and a Christian life; no need to quote early church fathers on this. "Here, then, is *utile, honestum,* and *necessarium,* to tie bishops in duty to kings; and a three-fold cord is not easily broken" (p. 10). So he complements his historical argument by asserting as simply and clearly as he can that *now* ecclesiastical rule by bishops is even more useful, honorable, and necessary; but Taylor takes them in reverse order and ends on the most practical, the most economical.

Are bishops necessary? Yes, for we are beset by contemporary Aerians and Acephali, the inevitable accompaniment of nonepiscopal disorder. The first Aerius, who was a heretical Arian, was never condemned as heretic by any church council for merely insisting that "a bishop and a priest are all one" (p. 196). Instead, he was laughed out of court for being ridiculous. One father said that his name Aerius was providential, for the "aerial spirits" flying around inside his head were obviously unclean ones. Everyone knows that a bishop and a priest are no more one than a subject and a king are one. As for the Acephali, in their days the churchmen who refused to be governed by their bishop were called *headless*, which is to say "witless." A bishop is as necessary to the church as a head is to a body. No need for a St. Paul or a St. Cyprian to tell us this. Yet Taylor does quote, in his summary, St. Clement, the disciple of St. Peter, as saying: "All priests, and clergymen, and people, and nations, and languages, that do not obey their bishop, shall be shut forth of the communion of holy church here, and of heaven hereafter" (p. 199). This language is too strong. "It runs high," Taylor observes, "but I cannot help it; I do but translate Rufinus as he before translated St. Clement." Taylor's style has changed in this second, more practical part of his argument. It is less stern and factual, more flowing, homely, and even jocose. A grimly humorous rejoinder, after the execution of Charles the First, to Taylor's wit on the Acephali was this: "Who's headless now?"

Granted, then, that bishops are necessary, are they deserving of honor? This question demands a review of "the guise of christendom in her spiritual heraldry." Bishops have always been men of learning and piety, doctors, scholars, great teachers, and administrators; the implication is that they still are. Custom has always granted them the highest titles of dignity, which set them above ordinary priests; the implication is that they should still be so set above presbyters.

Let us, finally, grant that bishops are *utile*, for what use can ever be made of this modern office called "lay elder"? Here Taylor's prose crackles with the Elizabethan vernacular of Samson's story as the champion accuses the Philistines of "ploughing with his own heifer" (Judg. 14:18):

> In this question of lay-elders the modern Aerians and Acephali do wholly mistake their own advantages; for whatever they object out of antiquity for the white and watery colours of lay-elders, is either a very misprision of their allegations, or else clearly abused in the use of them. For now-a-days they are only used to exclude and drive forth episcopacy; but then they misallege antiquity; for the men with whose heifers they would fain plough in this question were themselves bishops for the most part, and he that was not, would fain have been . . . (pp. 222–23).

Instead of giving us his usual "The sum is this," Taylor gets carried away with his conviction that a lay elder—compared with a bishop in necessity, honor, and actual usefulness—is unthinkable:

> The new office of a LAY-ELDER I confess I cannot comprehend in any reasonable proportion; his person, his quality, his office, his authority, his subordination, his commission hath made so many divisions and new emergent questions, and they none of them all asserted either by scripture or antiquity, that if I had a mind to leave the way of God and of the catholic church and run in pursuit of this meteor, I might quickly be amused, but should find nothing certain but a certainty of being misguided: therefore if not for conscience' sake, yet for prudence, *bonum est esse hic*, it is good to remain in the fold of Christ, under the guard and supravision of those shepherds Christ hath appointed, and which His sheep have always followed (p. 226).

The *tunc* and the *nunc*, episcopacy *for itself* and episcopacy *for us*, the conscience and the prudence, have been brought together.

Taylor wrote that last paragraph in 1641. In 1661 he himself was made a bishop in the Church of England. Given Parliament, Cromwell, the sequestration by law of the Anglican clergy, and the death of the king, it took faith on his part during eighteen years to believe that he had won his first published argument.

Liturgy (1646)

In 1646 Taylor published the second part (V, 259–314) of his polemic for the Anglican church, for its liturgy as opposed to extempore prayer so emphasized by the opposition. This early in his career of controversy he progressed from the outside of things to the inside, from polity and church government to its inner life, from the political science of ecclesiology to its mode of communing with God. "Liturgy" is the public common prayer of the whole church as opposed to the private ejaculatory petitions of individuals. As a reformed church that believed the church to be the community of all believers, the Anglican took special pains to "prove" this in emphasizing liturgy, the central portion of which is the celebration of the Holy Eucharist. Queen Elizabeth's injunction ordering the altar to be brought down from the chancel to the nave among the people for its celebration was a means of enabling them to take a greater share in the service. Anglicans usually refer not to "The Prayer-book" but to "The Book of Common Prayer," emphasizing the adjective. For this reason George Herbert in rebuilding his church had the reading pew from which he prayed with the people made of equal height with the pulpit on the opposite side: the liturgy and its "prayers in common" being of equal importance with the sermon.[9]

The Puritan faction in England emphasized the sermon as the climax of every service and in prayer depended upon the inspiration of the individual minister at the moment of delivery. To interdict *The Book of Common Prayer* was the purpose of the Westminster Assembly and Solemn League and Covenant, and to set up in its stead allowances for the minister to be moved in prayer and in sermon "by the Spirit." Its official publication entitled *The Directory for Publique Worship*, published January 3, 1645, Taylor immediately but anonymously countered with *A Discourse concerning Prayer Ex Tempore, or, by Pretence of the Spirit, in Justification of Authorized and Set-formes of Lyturgie* (1646). Now that the battle was joined, his book became so important that in 1649 Taylor not only enlarged it to twice its size and claimed authorship, but boldly dedicated it to the king on the eve of his execution.

Before going into his argument, however, it is important to pause for a few moments upon "the altar controversy" as part of the whole liturgical and antiliturgical debate. Whether the altar should be called an "altar" or a "table," whether it should be placed in the chancel or the nave or the narthex, and what part it should play in the sacrament of Holy Communion produced almost as thundering a spate of pamphlets as did the arguments on bishops and *The Book of Common Prayer*. A favorite verse among the Puritans to indicate their zealousness in preaching was Isa. 6:6 in which the prophet tells of the servant of the Seraphim fetching a coal from the altar and placing it upon his lips to give him the gift of prophesy. An anonymous "vicar of Grantham" in Lincolnshire had spoken for the holy use of the altar within the chancel, but this was answered in 1618 in a sermon by Samuel Ward called *A Coal from the Altar to Kindle the Holy Fire of Zeale*. Peter Heylin uses the same title *A Coale from the Altar* in 1636 to answer Ward. Then in 1637 an Anglican of Presbyterian persuasion published *The Holy Table, Name & Thing* from the Diocese of Lincolnshire. This immediately draws another response from the Anglican Heylin against "that schismaticall, factious, and seditious" party that brought forth such stuff as "was never uttered by Bostwicke, Layton, Burton, Prynne, or any pestilent Pasquill of the present, *ne dum* in any of the former times." Hence, in the same year, William Prynne, that arch-Puritan who had had his ears trimmed earlier for his part in *Histriomastix* and the theater controversy, published *A Quench-Coale; or, A Disquisition and Brief Inquirie in what place of the Church or*

Chancell the Lords-Table ought to be situate especially when the Sacrament is Administered. He fulminates against the "pretenses" of Richard Shelford, Edmund Reeve, John Pocklington, and Heylin's *A Coale from the Altar* which his own title is intended to extinguish forever. These, Prynne says, take their arguments from "the Iesuites, Priests, Papists, and anti-Christian Babilonish Sect of Rome. . . .[10] "Our church," he adds, "cashered Altars as Popish, Heathenish & Iewish."[11] The Anglican argument Prynne particularly answers here is that of John Pocklington's *Altare christianum; or the Dead Vicars Plea, Wherein the Vicar of Gr*[antham] *being dead, yet speketh and pleadeth out of Antiquity against him that hath broken down his Altar* (London, 1637). On February 2, 1641, Parliament sentenced Pocklington's Anglican tract to be publicly burned in London and at both universities by the common executioner.

What appears to be the earliest work we possess from Taylor's pen is a manuscript in the Queen's College library at Oxford called "On the Reverence due to the Altar," first printed by Heber (V, 317–38); another manuscript copy exists at the Bodleian. Heber believes that this piece was composed by Taylor when he was a fellow at All Souls, an appointment given him by Laud on January 14, 1636. On March 23, 1638, Taylor was presented by Juxon, bishop of London, to the living at Uppingham, Rutlandshire, the year which produced Taylor's first printed work, the Gunpowder Sermon. If this essay in the "altar controversy" is Taylor's, he must have written it in 1637, the very year that brought forth most of the various outbursts we have just quoted.[12]

The anonymous manuscript, in letter form addressed to an older person called "Sir," is evidently an initial effort in religious argumentation. The axiom is that God is to be worshiped; everything else must be proved. And the proof is historical, in periods chronologically arranged. The linking metaphor is "steps to the altar," the steps being those of time. In the Old Testament the sign of reverence from inferior to superior is invariably a "bowing down." All societies join the bodily action with the state of mind, so that to feel reverence and at the same time to bow or to kneel is no more than joining a *corde creditur* to an *ore fit confessio*. God is to be worshipped where He is most present. Just as we look at a man's face when we speak to him and not at his feet (though his feet are also "him"), so it is natural to render more reverence to the altar than (shall we say?) to the front porch. After the Old Testament, the manuscript continues, Christ taught reverence to the altar in his very first injunction: to leave your gift at the altar if you have malice in your heart, to forgive your brother first, and then return to make your sacrifice (Matt. 5:23–24). Then, in what will become Taylor's signature in disputation, the author says:

> The summe is this. Where God is present, there he is to be worshipped, and so according to the degree of his presence. He is specially present in Holy places, as Temples, Churches, Altars, therefore here are the places of our adoration. Such places are in the Gospell, as well as in the Law of Moses, for they are here both by the Law of Nature, and of the Gospell too (p. 325).

After Christ came the apostles, and after them the church fathers. All agree that special reverence is due the altar. "Well! *Sit anima mea cum Christianis*. I pray God I may go with the Christians," the author suddenly resolves, with a quotation attributed to the Moslem Averroes (p. 331). To pay such reverence as Christians have always paid to the altar is not to worship an image but to bow in obeisance to the Real Presence which dwells there (p. 337).

This argument on the altar has the stamp of Taylor's method, tone of Christian restraint, and style. It breaks occasionally into plain language such as: "How farre short this falls of the former, if it be driven home to its utmost issue, and bolted to the Bren [sifted to the bran], I ken not: doe you judge" (p. 336).[13] And it shows a mind already committed to the give-and-take of controversy. He quotes (p. 336) the great Puritan William Ames, who lived in exile in Holland, on cases of conscience: Amesius's *De Conscientia Eius Iure et Casibus* (Amstel., 1630). He quotes (p. 338) not only Bishop Jewel's reply to Harding that was published in London in 1609, but also, in a spirit of ecumenical scholarship, the Puritan Edward Dering's answer to Harding's answer to Bishop Jewel. Perhaps Archbishop Laud did not publish the piece, nor allow Taylor to claim it, because it was too mild for the altar controversy that raged in 1637.

We return now to Taylor's main argument in favor of liturgy published first in 1646 as an answer to the Presbyterian *Directory for Publique Worship*. In this, Taylor starts out mockingly like a scholastic to examine the *Directory* according to Aristotle's four secondary causes. Its efficient cause is unquestioned, for we all know who made it—Presbyterian divines Taylor was to tangle with, like Alexander Henderson and William Twisse. Its final cause also we may pass over since its end is certainly "the abolition and destruction of the Book of Common Prayer" (p. 260). As for the material cause, its matter is impossibly various. All we have left to inquire into is the formal cause, that is the shape of the argument it contains to substitute for the "set forms" of *The Book of Common Prayer* the prayers extempore which, to Taylor's mind, have by their nature no "form" at all.

At this point he characteristically breaks his argument into two segments based on two differing propositions the *Directory* offers for extempore prayer: (1) that all deliberation in prayer is to be avoided, and (2) that all deliberated prayers except "our own" are to be avoided. The first is frankly "separatist"; the second shows an anxiety to become the established "form" in place of the one England has had since Henry the Eighth and Archbishop Cranmer. Both principles go directly counter to the historical Anglican belief concerning the liturgy: that the prayer of the church (as differing from individual prayer) must be (1) edifying for the people, (2) structured psychologically and artistically, and (3) uniform for the sake of the unity of the church as the body of Christ. A substitution of extempore prayer (by definition dependent on individuals) for the carefully worked out *Book of Common Prayer* would be to risk boredom, accident, and variety among Christians.

So, Taylor counters the two propositions by asking two major questions anticipated by the last part of his title: *An Apology for Authorized and Set Forms of Liturgy against the Pretence of the Spirit for 1. Extempore prayer and 2. Forms of Private Composition.* The first question is whether it is better (the word *better* implying edification, order, and uniformity) for people gathered together in church to pray to God with or without deliberation. Obviously, it is better to deliberate prior to writing an important letter, or giving a lecture, or writing a book; then it is far better to offer deliberated prayers for the people to God than improvised ones.

The second question is more complex: whether it is better to retain the prayers in *The Book of Common Prayer* or to take only those which have been insisted upon by particular individuals in their anxiety to break away from set forms. These prayers are also "set," in a different sense and not nearly so well; they have not come down through the ages, nor been tested, though first composed by individuals, by the experience of countless worshippers praying together in communion. In fact, they are not "liturgy" in its real sense of "public worship" but merely the prayers of the Reverend Messrs. A, and B, and C.

As Taylor dealt with the first question by an appeal to common experience (seventeen pages), he deals with the second (thirty-six pages) by examining the grounds for the proposition advanced by a few men that only their own prayers should be offered in every religious assembly. The problem is one of the grounds for "liberty," which Taylor is already thinking about in preparation of his book published a year later, *The Liberty of Prophesying* (1647). He finds that *The Directory for Publique Worship* for this part of its discourse "relies wholly upon these two grounds: first, a liberty to use the variety of forms of prayer is more for the edification of the church; secondly, it is part of that liberty which the church hath, and part of the duty of the church to preserve the liberty of the Spirit in various forms" (p. 279). Especially for the central sacrament of Christian worship, the Holy Eucharist, the opposition will have to prove that their *Directory* is more edifying, more carefully structured, and more familiar by dint of repetition to thousands of communicants in thousands of churches than the liturgy of *The Book of Common Prayer*.

Lest we forget that the words "liturgy" and "communion" are inseparable, Taylor again reminds us:

> Before I descend to consideration of the particulars I must premise this, that the gift or ability of prayer given to the church is used either in public or private, and that which is fit enough for one is inconvenient in the other; and although a liberty in private may be for edification of good people when it is piously and discreetly used, yet in the public if it were indifferently permitted it would bring infinite inconvenience, and become intolerable, as a sad experience doth too much verify (pp. 279–80).

In private prayer, then, we may grant the Spirit all the liberty it needs, but that very liberty which in private fulfills the particular needs of each individual must, in public, be sacrificed.

The first ground, then, for premeditated prayers of private composition in the church is that a liberty to use a variety of forms gains more edification for the people than do set forms. This ground, Taylor has shown, is false in that it is only a "pretence of the Spirit." He consequently substitutes for it "those grounds of religion and reason upon which public liturgy relies, and by the strength of which it is to be justified, against all opposition and pretences" (p. 284). These grounds are greatly expanded in the second edition of 1649 from that of 1646, as Taylor laboriously comes to "eleventhly," "twelfthly," and "thirteenthly."

"In the next place," he continues, "we must consider the next great objection, that in set forms of prayer we restrain and confine the blessed Spirit . . ." (p. 305), and the second ground in the *Directory* for privately written prayers in public places. Taylor argues here, as we would expect, that *their* prayers actually are more restraining of the Spirit than those of *The Book of Common Prayer.* They restrain a body of worshipers rather than freeing it, whereas "set forms" actually liberate. Christ took it upon Himself to *restrain* the individual spirits of His twelve differing disciples when He taught them to "pray after this manner: Our Father which art in heaven . . ." (p. 307). Paradoxically, this set form freed them sufficiently to be able to pray together to God. "To sum up all," Taylor concludes,

> If it be pretended that in the liturgy of the church of England, which was composed with much art and judgment, by a church that hath as much reason to be confident she hath the spirit and "gift of prayer" as any single person hath; and each learned man that was at its first composition can as much prove that he had the Spirit as the objectors now-a-days . . . ; if, I say, it be pretended that there are many errors and inconveniences both in the order and in the matter of the Common Prayer-Book, made by such men, with so much industry: how much more and with how much greater reason may we all dread the inconveniences and disorders of *ex tempore* and "conceived" prayers; where respectively there is neither conjunction of heads, nor premeditation, nor industry, nor method, nor art, nor any of those things, or at least not in the same degree, which were like to have exempted the Common Prayer-Book from errors and disorders (p. 311).

No particular person is to be trusted to offer prayer in public with his private spirit to God either without premeditation or because *he* considered it. "An unlearned man is not to be trusted, and a wise man dare not trust himself: he that is ignorant cannot, he that is knowing will not" (p. 314).

This ends Jeremy Taylor's first controversy, which he undertook for the "liberty" of the Church of England between 1642 and 1646. We find him arguing with erudition, wisdom, and rhetorical skill. And though neither argument shows him as merely serving his superiors, the second is far greater than the first. The argument for episcopacy, based initially on shaky Biblical grounds, falls far behind the ingenious, often profound, and finally witty argument in favor of the liturgy.

Characteristically, he thus demonstrates early his fondness for encompassing dichotomies. His argument for bishops breaks into two halves, which he later joins, episcopacy *in itself* and episcopacy *for us*. His other argument for the church again breaks into two parts if we count the early manuscript: reverence due to the altar and the advantages of *The Book of Common Prayer*. The latter argument divides itself into two major questions called for by the title page, which parallel the two parties in the Westminster Assembly who opposed the Anglican "set forms." Finally, in the very last part of his last argument, he examines two grounds for the liberty that one of those parties demands for substituting its private prayers for the public worship.

Hence the shapes Taylor gives to his arguments are inseparable from the substance of what he is arguing.

Golden Grove and the Argument for Freedom of Religious Opinion

III

The War in Wales

Bishop Heber, among modern biographers, began the tradition that Taylor was captured by Parliamentary troops at the skirmish before Cardigan Castle, which occurred on February 4, 1644. He assumed, however, that being captured meant also that he was imprisoned. "How long Taylor remained a prisoner, and on what terms and by whose interest he was released, there are now small hopes of recovering," he writes (I, xxviii). Yet he is aware of the improbability of Taylor's being imprisoned for as long an interval as that between the skirmish before Cardigan Castle and the publication of *The Liberty of Prophesying* (1647), "the time necessary to collect books, and . . . to prepare for the press such an essay as that to which he chiefly [this was written in 1821] owes his fame . . ." (I, xxvii).

Heber was led to his information on the "imprisonment" by a manuscript note of Mr. Bonney to "Whitelocke's Memorials, p. 130." Bulstrode Whitelocke (1605–75), a St. John's man, Laudian Anglican, and Oxford lawyer, took the Parliamentary side in the Civil War but refused to prosecute Laud; and, though a member of the committee to plan the trial of the king, would take no part in the sentence. His posthumously published "history" was entitled *Memorials of the English*

*Affairs: or, An Historical Account of what passed from the be-
ginning of the Reign of King Charles the First, to King Charles
the Second His Happy Restauration . . . London, Nath. Ponder,
1682.* Under "Anno 1644" but without further date, he writes:
"Letters from Captain *Swanley* informed, that Major General
Laughern took the Town of Cardigan in Wales upon surrender, but the Castle holding out obstinately, he made a breach
with his great Ordnance, and in three days took it by storm,
and in it 200 officers and Souldiers, with their Armes, and much
Plunder" (p. 119). A few pages later (p. 125) he describes
how, when Royalist General Gerard besieged Cardigan Castle
to take it back, Lieutenant Colonel Poole, who was holding it
for Parliament, sent for Laugharne; this astute military man
shot an arrow into the castle with a note telling Poole to sally
out at the moment that he (Laugharne) would attack. The ex-
ploit was successful, and among the Royalists captured in this
pincer attack, Whitelocke says, was "Dr. Taylor." Jeremy
Taylor, as a chaplain to the Royalist troops in Wales, may
well have been rounded up in this maneuver, but Whitelocke
does not say that he was put into prison. Prisoners of war were
often exchanged on the spot, or granted amnesty on condition
of "good behavior."

That Taylor was not imprisoned at this time at Cardigan
or elsewhere appears more probable from his dedication of
The Liberty of Prophesying to his former patron of Uppingham days, Sir Christopher Hatton. The famous opening deserves quoting in full once more:

> My Lord, In this great storm which has dashed the vessel
> of the church all in pieces, I have been cast upon the coast
> of Wales, and in a little boat thought to have enjoyed that
> rest and quietness which in England in a greater I could
> not hope for. Here I cast anchor, and thinking to ride
> safely, the storm followed me with so impetuous violence,
> that it broke a cable, and I lost my anchor; and here again
> I was exposed to the mercy of the sea, and the gentleness
> of an element that could neither distinguish things nor
> persons. And but that He who stilleth the raging of the

seas, and the noise of His waves, and the madness of His
people, had provided a plank for me, I had been lost to all
the opportunities of content or study. But I know not
whether I have been preserved by the courtesies of my
friends, or the gentleness and mercies of a noble enemy:
[Acts 28:2, quoted in Greek—"The rough islanders treated
us with uncommon kindness; because it was cold and had
started to rain, they lit a bonfire and made us all wel-
come"] (V, 341).[1]

Taylor talks here not of imprisonment but of rescue, warmth,
and opportunity to study. The noble enemy must have been
Major General Laugharne; and the kind friends, Earl and
Countess of Carbery of Golden Grove.

Rowland Laugharne, according to Clarendon, was "a
gentleman of good extraction and a fair fortune in those coun-
tries, who had been bred a page under the Earl of Essex. . . .
[He] was first engaged in the rebellion, as many other gentle-
men had been, without wishing ill to the King."[2] After Cardigan, he reduced Carew and Roach Castles in early March,
1644; Carmarthenshire fell to him in October, 1645; and in
February, 1646, he relieved Cardiff Castle, and took Aber-
ystwyth on April 14, 1646. In 1648, however, he left the Parliamentary side and declared "for the King."

Richard Vaughan, second earl of Carbery, had been a
member of Parliament from Carmarthenshire from 1624–26,
and again in 1628–29. Created Knight of the Bath at Charles's
coronation, he became lieutenant general of the royal forces in
Carmarthenshire, Cardiganshire, and Pembroke, but showed
little spirit to force his men to fight against Laugharne. When
he lost Pembroke, he resigned his commission and retired to his
Welsh ancestral estate, Golden Grove. Here, distrusted by
both sides, he remained for the duration of the war under leni-
ent house arrest, with Jeremy Taylor as his family chaplain.
His love for his first wife (his second wife as a young girl had
played the part of the Lady in Milton's *Comus*), for his lands,
and for his chaplain are well known. His notorious political
ambiguity, however, perhaps best appears in his advice to his

33

son Frank in a "courtesy book" written in the late summer of 1651. Its opening ship metaphor resembles Taylor's in the dedication to *The Liberty of Prophesying:*

> First be sure to ballast your selfe well by calling in to your ayde all the advantages of Learning, Arte and Experience; Then consider how to fitt your Sayles to the Bulke of your Vessell, lest you proue a Slugge or ouersett. And because Commonwealths haue theire shelues and Rockes, therefore gett the Skill of Coasting and shifting your Sayles, I mean to arriue at your Endes by Compassings and an honest complyance.[3]

Taylor, a chaplain in Wales in 1644–45, could do little to mend the now hopeless military situation, and he may have been warned, as part of the price of protection, to stay out of controversy. Besides, he needed peace to devote himself to the greater cause of religion and reason. Loving his church and steeped in its history of reasonableness that linked bishops, people, and sovereign, as indeed he had argued in 1642, Taylor became convinced of the fruitlessness of violence in maintaining any ecclesiastical and political establishment. On Carbery's estate, while the war waged on in the rest of Wales and across the Severn in Somersetshire, Taylor finished *The Liberty of Prophesying*, the first great work of his Golden Grove period, a period which marks the high point in his literary career.

The Liberty of Prophesying (1647)

The initial words of its title in Greek are *Theologia Eklektike*, an immediate indication of its spirit. Printed for R. Royston at the Angel in Ivie-lane, the book has a handsome frontispiece by Will Marshall showing a radiant sun and under it twelve apostles each with a little lambent flame above his head. It was Will Marshall who did the frontispiece of the man falling from the rock for Browne's *Religio Medici* in 1642, and the famous kneeling figure of Charles the First for *Eikon Basilike*. In copied Greek, probably as little understood by the same artist as that which he engraved for the infamous portrait of Milton, the emblem for *The Liberty of Prophesying* has a quotation from 1 Cor. 14:31: "That ye may all prophesy one by one."

The twenty-three page letter to Sir Christopher Hatton which introduces it is more than a dedication: it performs four distinct functions. First, it justifies Taylor's writing such a book in the midst of the Civil War. Though Christ's doctrine is one of peace especially among those who profess His name, animosities are at too high a pitch merely to harangue: one must surrender the present in order to argue at length, with reason and in writing, to save the future.

Second, the letter sets the tone or temper of the argument and of the conduct of any Christian inquiry into truth, which is its end. This temper can best be summarized by quoting a single sentence written to Hatton, but its spirit pervades the whole: "Only let not men be hasty in calling every disliked opinion by the name of heresy; and when they have resolved that they will call it so, let them use the erring person like a brother, not beat him like a dog, or convince him with a gibbet, or vex him out of his understanding and persuasions" (p. 354).

Third, to anticipate all possible objections, the letter clearly states Taylor's grounds and sources. For one side to kill, maim, and persecute the other in an effort to enforce its views is, to Taylor, "unblessed, unsuccessful, and unreasonable" (p. 352): that is, opposed to God, to man's best interests, and that faculty of reason which links the Creator to his creation. These are the grounds on which Taylor based all his arguments, for he was at once religious, practical, and rational. His authority will come from the words of Christ, the writings of the apostles, and of the church fathers during the first three centuries of the Christian era. Familiar to us from Taylor's previous argument, these grounds and sources are, of course, not peculiar to Taylor, but are the standard of the Elizabethan and Jacobean Anglican apologists.

Finally, the "Dedication" explains the last part of the title page—the "just limits and temper" of "the liberty of prophesying," or exceptions to the rule of freedom in Biblical interpretation. If his grounds are religious, rational, and practical, he must exclude from toleration those opinions which violate the glory and honor of God, which seem to be based on an irrational exegesis of text, and which result merely in domestic and civil disturbance. To tolerate these would be to grant license, not liberty, since liberty entails responsibility. As he was to say in his preface to *A Collection of Offices* in 1658, it is unsafe both to grant absolute liberty in reading Scripture and to deny that liberty, for "reason and religion will chide us in the first, reason and experience in the other" (VII, 242). Again, in his dedication to Hatton of the 1657 volume containing a reissue of *The Liberty of Prophesying*, he called attention to the fact that to keep "unreasonable pretenders" from entering "the gate of toleration" he had placed guards in front of it "allowing none to enter here that speak against the apostles' creed, or weakened the hands of government, or were enemies to good life" (V, 3). Thus, there can be no toleration of opinions which are "against the foundation of faith, or contrary to good life and the laws of obedience, or destructive to human society and the public and just interest of bodies politic" (p. 346).

This is to serve God and to serve man, but there are already, always have been and always will be, thousands of differing opinions on what is necessary to believe for salvation and what is best for our life on earth. Many of these, being speculative, indeterminate, curious, and unnecesary, are harmless as long as only God is our judge; but when they are made articles of a fighting faith and their harborers attempt to force others to believe them or to suffer for disbelief, then it is everybody's business. Right reason must prevail in distinguishing true from false, necessary from unnecessary; reason thus used will lead to a firmer faith and a greater charity. To begin with, we might call things by their right names, not "all opinions by the name of religion, and superstructures by the name of fundamental articles, and all fancies by the glorious appellative of faith" (p. 348). *The Liberty of Prophesying* is a dissuasive from tyranny, not an encourager of free thought.

36

This brings us to the book itself. Like so many seventeenth-century discourses, it too falls into two great halves. Faith and hope enter the first part: charity, the second—like Browne's *Religio Medici*. Articles of belief enter the first part; and rules of conduct based on that belief, the second—like Milton's *De Doctrina Christiana*. Taylor's argument, again, like some medical treatises of the period and later, consists of diagnosis and cure. It is also one of means and ends. It is characterized by innumerable divisions into two, constant oppositions, and interactions between two terms to form final syntheses—the pattern we have defined as the Platonic-Christian dichotomy.

Though disjunctives also are plentiful in his argument, Taylor's *The Liberty of Prophesying* as a whole has the shape of this dichotomous, oppositional, but also hierarchical and encompassing mode of thought. The great break into two large segments of discourse comes at page 514 of the Heber-Eden edition (Vol. V). Following the two commands of Christ, first comes faith, and then love. Part I deals with belief and disbelief; part II, with an orderly and pious life. The major dichotomy is made explicit in a paragraph which forms the summary of part I and the transition to part II, that is, a key paragraph at midpoint:

> So that now, since no error neither for itself nor its consequents is to be charged as criminal upon a pious person; since no simple error is a sin, nor does condemn us before the throne of God; since He is so pitiful to our crimes that He pardons many *de toto et integro,* in all makes abatement for the violence of temptation and the surprisal and invasion of our faculties, and therefore much less will demand of us an account for our weaknesses; and since the strongest understanding cannot pretend to such an immunity and exemption from the condition of men as not to be deceived and confess its weakness: it remains we enquire what deportment is to be used towards persons of a differing persuasion, when we are (I do not say doubtful of a proposition, but) convinced that he that differs from us is in error: for this was the first intention and the last end of this discourse (p. 514).

37

Again, on the next to the last page of *The Liberty of Prophesying* Taylor writes:

> The sum of all is this: there is no security in any thing or to any person but in the pious and hearty endeavours of a good life, and neither sin nor error does impede it from producing its proportionate and intended effect; because it is a direct deletery to sin, and an excuse to errors by making them innocent and therefore harmless. And indeed this is the intendment and design of faith. For (that we may join both ends of this discourse together) therefore certain articles are prescribed to us and propounded to our understanding, so that we might be supplied with instructions, with motives and engagements to incline and determine our wills to the obedience of Christ. So that obedience is just so consequent to faith, as the acts of will are to the dictates of the understanding (p. 603).

In these two key passages the pairs of terms or stylistic doublets forming the major dichotomy are clearly restated. Throughout the entire discourse they appear and reappear in many different forms and combinations: understanding and deportment; cognition and will; means and ends; past and present; internal and external; reasonable and effectual; faith and piety; belief and charity; cause and effect; diagnosis and prescription; intention and result; thinking and acting; grounds and conclusions; foundation and superstructure; wisdom and justice; doctrine and practice; love of God and love of man. To put each pair of terms in the proper hierarchy and to work for their systasis is to achieve Christian liberty.

Each of these two main parts is again subdivided into two very similar subsegments. The first part splits between the general nature of faith and of heresy, and "The result of all is this: . . ." (p. 494), practical considerations. Similarly, the second large part divides into, first, more immediate grounds (p. 514) than part I did, and: ". . . it remains that we reduce this doctrine to practical conclusions" (p. 536). Like Plato's famous "twice-bisected line" near the end of the sixth book of the *Republic*, then, we get a kind of four-part proportion of

38

A:B:C:D, progressing from the most general down to the most practical, the *two* test cases of toleration—Anabaptists and Roman Catholics. Oppositions between dividing terms and segments are so set up as to allow constant interaction between them until the reader is convinced of the necessity of toleration by the "not-only-but-also" encompassing dialectic of ends and means. To Taylor faith is no virtue in and for itself but only as a means to obedience. Obedience is nothing in itself; it is only a means to Christ. And what is Christ except the means God has given us to Himself? This is the "economy of God."

The problem to be explored is stated in the first sentence. The infinite variety of religious opinions has been impeding the advancement of Christ's kingdom for some time, and no one has yet discovered a good way to deal with it. Some (the Roman Catholics?) propose a single guide by persuasion; but, like inept medical practice, this intends a cure for the wrong part: it hopes to achieve unity of action without getting at unity of mind. Others (the Presbyterians and Independents?) hope to establish a single rule by sheer power, which again treats the symptoms rather than the disease (p. 365). Both of these attempts, failing to set up a hierarchy of opinions, dispose their rewards and punishments as though opinions all bore the same consequence. Yet, in the one, insisting that a deathbed repentance can instantly assure salvation is more heinous than a belief in Purgatory; and, in the other, clinging to predestination has more serious effect than the personal like or dislike of a private mass (p. 366). The persistent variety of opinions in itself is not pernicious, but the lack of charity that arises from this failure to distinguish is (p. 367). Thus love is not merely emotional and reason intellectual, but both are both.

"All these errors and mischiefs must be discovered and cured, and that's the purpose of this discourse" (p. 368), which is plain dealing enough. Upon examination many of them will be found (1) not to be revealed (faith), (2) if they are found in the Bible they are often obscure or irrelevant (reason), and often (3) being not necessary they carry no compulsion to act (practice). We cannot all be of one mind, but every opinion

39

should not become an article of faith justifying civil disobedience, persecution, torture, and murder:

> All these mischiefs proceed not from this, that all men are not of one mind, for that is neither necessary nor possible, but that every opinion is made an article of faith, every article is a ground of a quarrel, every quarrel makes a faction, and every faction is zealous, and all zeal pretends for God, and whatsoever is for God cannot be too much: we by this time are come to that pass, we think we love not God except we hate our brother, and we have not the virtue of religion unless we persecute all religions but our own; for lukewarmness is so odious to God and man, that we proceeding furiously upon these mistakes, by supposing we preserve the body we destroy the soul of religion, or by being zealous for faith, or which is all one, for that which we mistake for faith, we are cold in charity, and so lose the reward of both (p. 368).

From this point Taylor must examine, first, the nature of real faith, and then, since wherever there is an orthodoxy there must also be a heresy, he must define the nature of heresy. Though it may be ironical that he devotes only thirteen paragraphs to the one and forty-one to the other, the very disproportion becomes part of his argument that truth is clear, simple, and unified, whereas error, as in Donne's third satire, is invariably muddled, complex, and multifarious.

The fundamental article of faith among all Christians is that Christ was crucified for our sins and was raised from the dead to be a perpetual redeemer of mankind. Taylor would be willing to settle for "the one thing necessary" on the experience of Mary (p. 369), who stayed away from the kitchen in order to listen to the Lord and so believed that her brother Lazarus would rise: "Jesus said, 'I am the resurrection and I am the life. If a man has faith in me, even though he die, he shall come to life; and no one who is alive and has faith shall ever die. Do you believe this?' 'Lord, I do,' she answered; 'I now believe that you are the Messiah, the son of God who was to come into the world' " (John 11:25–27). Or even more simply, a full creed (p. 369) is that of St. Peter: "We believe and are sure that thou art Christ, the son of the living God" (Matt. 16:16). The pathway to heaven is steep and narrow enough without placing further stumbling blocks in it (p. 371). Only those articles which can be clearly deduced from these central propositions of Christ and the apostles are necessary to belief, and these were formulated for all in the Apostles' Creed.

Any man in his private conscience may give whatsoever interpretations he pleases to its various parts, but no more should be "pressed on others as an article of faith" than the creed itself (p. 374). If indeed it was the foundation for the apostles and for the church fathers of the first three centuries, then it still is, for though superstructures have been erected upon it since, a foundation does not alter with time (p. 377). "Whatever private men's opinions were, yet till the Nicene council [A.D. 325] the rule of faith was entire in the apostles' creed; and provided they retained that, easily they broke not the unity of faith, however differing opinions might possibly commence in such things in which a liberty were better suffered, than prohibited with a breach of charity" (p. 395). So much for faith.

Now the nature of heresy must be examined by analogy with the nature of faith (p. 378). In both there are both cognition and will: faith is not merely a matter of truth, nor error a mere matter of will since love is first necessary to faith and in its opposite an error of knowing can impel the will to wander. The history of the articles of belief shows that charity towards those who opposed them was just as important as the articles themselves. For certainly the question of circumcision by the Jews was solemnly argued as denying them the appellative of Christian as it was applied to the Gentiles, yet no anathema was ever leveled if circumcision were held innocently. The great example is St. Paul himself; God had mercy on him because though "he was not convinced in his understanding of the truth of the way which he persecuted, he in the meanwhile remain[ed] in that incredulity not out of malice or ill ends, but the mistakes of humanity and a pious zeal" (p. 381).

Thus the early history of error is full of examples of heretics being self-condemned, that is, not irrationally or uncharitably censored by authority of church or state but inviting punishment through their adding to their error of understanding the error of impiety, obstinacy, and misled zeal to form a sect. In St. Paul's words, "Evil men and seducers shall wax worse and worse, deceiving and being deceived" [2 Tim. 3:13] (p. 385). Hence, "The further the succession went from the apostles, the more forward men were in numbering heresies, and that upon slighter and more uncertain grounds" (p. 389), the horrendous proliferation beginning in the fourth century of the Christian era.

Because we would expect the history of error to be more compendious than that of truth, we need not detail the numerous "heresies" in Taylor's account at this point. Suffice it to remark in a single example, the comparison between St. Cyprian and St. Stephen (pp. 396–97), how Taylor consistently joins charity to faith and hope, and action to belief and unbelief: "A wicked person in his error becomes heretic, when the good man in the same error shall have all the rewards of faith" (p. 397). St. Cyprian's way of dealing with heretics is preferable to that of St. Stephen because the former charitably judged the intention of promulgating the article rather than the article itself, erroneous though it was. Lest we lose his thread in a long history of error, Taylor colors it red for us; he begins with a phrase which by now is a hallmark of his polemic style:

> The sum of this discourse is this: if we take an estimate of the nature of faith from the dictates and promises evangelical and from practice apostolical, the nature of faith and its integrity consists in such propositions which make the foundation of hope and charity, that which is sufficient to make us to do honour to Christ, and to obey Him, and to encourage us in both; and this is completed in the apostles'

creed. And since contraries are of the same extent, heresy is to be judged by its proportion and analogy to faith, and that is heresy only which is against faith. Now because faith is not only a precept of doctrines but of manners and holy life, whatsoever is either opposite to an article of creed, or teaches ill life, that's heresy; but all those propositions which are extrinsical to these two considerations, be they true or false, make not heresy, nor the man a heretic; and therefore however he may be an erring person, yet he is to be used accordingly, pitied and instructed, not condemned and excommunicated; and this is the result of the first ground, the consideration of the nature of FAITH and HERESY (p. 409).

But there is still an important consideration in this first part of the discourse before Taylor, in the middle of the Civil War, can lay out his first set of practical rules for religious behavior. As an Anglican he has been applying reason to history, which he shares with the Roman Catholic; as a Protestant, however, who believes that all things necessary to salvation are found in the Bible, he must now apply reason to its interpretation (pp. 409–514), particularly as most of the difficulties of the time arose from post-Reformation zealots who founded and promulgated their sects on particular passages of Scripture. If it is true that every article of the Apostles' Creed is Biblical and if it is true that those articles contain all that distinguishes a Christian from a pagan, then Taylor can concentrate on those indeterminable points in Scripture which have become, since the fourth century, the cause of proliferation in articles of belief and in the methods of handling them. The "gifts of prophecy" are given to or taken by those who interpret the Scriptures, and just what "liberty of prophesying" can any one justly claim? The Bible is before us, and Christ's central commands are perfectly clear. As St. Paul (p. 410) wrote to Timothy: "Every inspired scripture has its use for teaching the truth and refuting error, or for reformation of manners and discipline in right living, so that the man who belongs to God may be efficient and equipped for good work of every kind" [2 Tim. 3:16].

The fact is, however, that except for the few "clear and necessary" articles gathered from the Bible into the Apostles' Creed, agreement on what the Bible means is made utterly impossible by two enormous considerations, one internal and the other external. One is the nature of the Scriptures themselves in their linguistic and grammatical form as well as in their figurative and anagogical modes of expression. The books have undergone a human history of variant texts and multiple transscriptions (p. 411). Also, "When the grammatical sense is found out we are many times never the nearer . . ." (p. 414), for non-literal expressions like "I am the vine" and "I am the door" can be quibbled over by exegetes forever. Even similar expressions in different parts of the Bible must be given different meanings from their particular contexts. Some of these in their literal and singular interpretations have uncharitably divided whole segments of Christendom; for example, the texts which "forbid" the Anabaptists from baptizing none but "believers" (that is, adults) and the Church of Rome from allowing the very young to partake of the Holy Eucharist (p. 418)—the two sects of Christianity which will become Taylor's final examples for insisting upon a qualified liberty of prophesying.

That "these considerations are taken from the nature of scripture itself," Taylor continues (p. 421), makes it mandatory to employ external aids in the interpretation of all but those central and necessary points. Again with characterisitc dichotomy, these external aids are *two*, neither to be trusted absolutely: public announcement by councils and church leaders to ratify tradition, and private individual reason. Before Taylor is through, scepticism forces him, as it did Browne and Dryden, into a fideistic acceptance, once more, of the Apostles' Creed and the established civil order. In this respect he shares the sceptical tradition with Montaigne, one of whose favorite verbs, incidentally, *mesnager* ("to husband"), is a reminder of the economy of God. Montaigne did his best to stay out of the religious wars in France, and sought for liberty not in the doctrinaire and forceful imposition of a reformed religion but in the already established, socially workable, and consequently not completely logical religion that France had always had.

What human external aids to interpret Scripture can be so infallible as to justify St. Bartholomew massacres in France or, in England, parliamentary rebellion against king and bishop? The power of a "New Model Army"? Encyclicals of various popes? The scholastic wranglings of confuting church fathers? The majority votes of various church councils? A hundred such cannot make two and two equal five for a person who insists they are four. Taylor is long on each one of these points, but lest we miss his intention he places them all in another neat summary:

> The result of all is this: Since it is not reasonable to limit and prescribe to all men's understandings by any external rule in the interpretation of difficult places of scripture, which is our rule; since no man nor company of men is secure from error, or can secure us that they are free from malice, interest, and design; and since all the ways by which we usually are taught, as tradition, councils, decretals, &c., are very uncertain in their matter, in their authority, in their being legitimate and natural, and many of them certainly false, and nothing certain but the divine authority of scripture, in which all that is necessary is plain, and much of that that is not necessary, is very obscure, intricate, and involved: either we must set up our rest only upon articles of faith and plain places, and be incurious of other obscurer revelations (which is a duty for persons of private understandings and of no public function) or if we will search further (to which in some measure the guides of others are obliged) it remains we enquire how men may determine themselves so as to do their duty to God and not to disserve the church, that every such man may do what he is bound to in his personal capacity, and as he relates to the public as a public minister (p. 494).

The reiterated dichotomies in this key passage which is a negative summary are more of the disjunctive Ramistic type than that kind which allows a systasis and fulfillment of the opposites to form the more perfect third. The whole discourse will be divided into theory and practice. The first part, so far, has been divided into faith and heresy and problems of reading the Bible. Reading the Bible brings up internal and external difficulties. The internal difficulties consist of textual and rhetorical obstacles to interpreting passages that are not plain but merely obscure. The external Biblical aids are either decisions on meaning made by public bodies or determination of meaning through individual reason.

Thus by disjunctive pairs of terms we are reduced, in this first largely theoretical half, to REASON—forced, as it were, to determine by its lone aid the meaning of those parts of the Bible which are obscure. From this point we learn, not so much by what Taylor says as by the way he argues, the meaning of "right reason." For now Taylor begins to conjoin pairs; he that follows his reason, led *not only* by natural arguments *but also* by divine revelation, has the surest guide.

Yet before this can come about, we must be shown how inadequate the merely natural human reason is. One of Taylor's examples of the church's failure to follow it makes an interesting link between the Council of Trent and Vatican II of our own day. Taylor mentions the obligatory decrees denying "the restitution of priests to their liberty of marriage, the use of the chalice, and the mass in the vulgar tongue"—all "just and reasonable demands made by . . . the ablest divines among them" but outlawed by the sixteenth-century council (p. 495). The very inadequacy of reason makes the practical end fully as important as the means. Even bad opinions, undergirded by the best human reason we can furnish, must be tolerated so long as they enjoin innocent persons (1) to promote the glory of God and (2) to lead a good and holy life (p. 513). "Let the error be never so great, so it be not against an article of creed, if it be simple and hath no confederation with the personal iniquity of the man, the opinion is as innocent as the person, though perhaps as false as he is ignorant . . ." (p. 511).

This must be our only mode of behavior when we consider the great variety of opinion that arises from the fallibility of reason itself. There follows a convincing array of "vulgar errors" all committed by their "rational" proponents (pp. 499–510). St. Peter's vision of the sheet let down from heaven filled with beasts and the heavenly command to "kill and eat" has meant to some a vacation from fish diet and to others a justification to murder "heretical" princes. Again, zeal can charge, despite reason, in any direction it pleases: look at the incredibly lengthy controversy concerning graven images. Sometimes we think we are reasonable when we are impelled merely by our physical and psychological condition, so that an opinion is fiercely defended on grounds of good or bad fortune. Even education, the mother of rational minds, "is so great and so invincible a prejudice" that we are prone to think the earliest things we learned must be the truest—like the adage in Frost's poem, "Good fences make good neighbors." Taylor's example here (p. 506) is the shameful events in the trial of Urban Grandier and "the devils of Loudun" made famous in our day by the late Aldous Huxley. Again, rational minds think they do honor to one of God's saints only as they invent miracles; Sir Thomas More tells how St. Augustine was persuaded that a story Lucian scoffs at was actually true (p. 507). If the best minds make mistakes like these, what of the more numerous weak understandings? They often proceed in the name of reason on a proverb or a false definition to build whole systems of "truth." And yet, "by their fruits ye shall know them," Christ said, and if the fruits of any opinion be not evil, then the tree that bears them should not be cut down.

Thus the sceptical recognition of the limits of reason leads Taylor into tolerating opinions (not evil acts) which are based on it; but more importantly, his scepticism defines the true grounds for determining religious truth. Such external guides as councils, popes, church fathers can only furnish evidence which reason, after all, must judge; and reason can judge by its only instruments, good or bad grounds. Good grounds are a good and pious life, which opens us to the will of God, coupled with a rational decision on the *more probable* of two competing "truths." Thus "reason" becomes "right reason"— a Renaissance voice from pagan antiquity and Christianity which seemed to have been silenced after the Council of Dort (1618) condemned the Dutch Arminians for using "rational" arguments in their opposition to Calvinism.

This brings Taylor to the end of the first half of his argument, that half consisting of doctrine, and leads him into his second half (p. 514) on how we should conduct ourselves toward people whose opinions still differ from our own: the two halves initiated by the title page—"The liberty of prophesying, its *just limits* and *temper*." The nature of the argument demands that these two parts be not mutually exclusive; as we have seen, there is practice in doctrine, and in the rest of his essay doctrine will reappear with practice. He introduces his second part with the marginal heading, "Of the deportment to be used towards persons disagreeing, and the reason why they are not to be punished with death."

The fundamental rule for behavior is: "No Christian is to be put to death for his opinion, which does not teach impiety or blasphemy" (p. 514). Again, the exceptions are stated: only those opinions can be thus tolerated which do not in themselves lead to a denial of the fundamental precepts of Christianity (as in the Apostles' Creed), or which do not militate against a charitable public or private life. The term "opinion" is in itself a proviso since no one whose opinion leads him to deny God or to lead an immoral life is indulging merely in opinion but in acts. Murder, arson, theft, and backbiting are acts which must be dealt with quite apart from Taylor's whole plea for toleration. If in the social "progress" we have made since his day we are still struggling to learn that corporal punishment cannot cure even these ills, how right Taylor was to argue in his time that no man should ever be whipped, maimed, scalded, or pressed between stones to change his opinion.

Part of his recommendation for action is that used by Gamaliel when the Jews wished to persecute Christ. If the one we persecute is really right in his opinion, then we are fighting God and the opinion will prevail as truth despite what we do. If the opinion is really wrong, then we make a martyr of his person and mislead others to his side. How can any one be sure? After listing ten reasons for never persecuting any one whose opinions merely differ from ours, Taylor gives us another of his unadorned almost vernacular sentences: "You may as well cure the colic by brushing a man's clothes, or fill his belly with a syllogism" (p. 522). Persecuting such people is simply illogical, impractical, and a misuse of the principle of means and ends.

The practicality of his single rule is demonstrated by a brief history of persecution. No record exists of the persecution of people whose religious opinions differed in the times of the apostles, nor indeed during the three centuries which followed. With minute citation of texts of the early fathers, Taylor notes that Priscillian was the first to be condemned to death for heresy and that by the tyrant Maximus. Thus only as collateral designs, special interests, and particular passions entered into the history of religious opinion did persecution begin: "As men had ends of their own and not of Christ's, as they receded from their duty and religion from its purity, as Christianity began to be compounded with interests and blended with temporal designs, so men were persecuted for their opinions" (p. 528). The saddest corollary of this is the arrogation of spiritual powers by civil governors and of temporal powers by those of the church to bring about the elimination of disagreeing persons. "So that," Taylor concludes, ". . . in the best times, amongst the best men, when there were fewer temporal ends to be served, when religion and the pure and simple designs of Christianity were only to be promoted, in those times and amongst such men no persecution was actual, nor persuaded nor allowed, towards disagreeing persons" (pp. 527–28). Thus Taylor was a reader of history, particularly the early history of the church and the fathers of the first three centuries. As he said in a sermon towards the end of his life: "For it is otherwise in theology than it is in other learnings. The experiments of philosophy [natural science] are rude at first, and the observations weak, and the principles unproved; and he that made the first lock was not so good a workman as we have nowadays: but in christian religion they that were first were best, because God and not man was the teacher; and ever since that, we have been unlearning the wise notices of pure religion, and mingling them with human notices and human interest" (VIII, 538). Christ was closest to God, the apostles to Christ, and the fathers of the first three centuries to them.

This brings him in his practical section to the vexed problem of church versus state. Once more, the effects of opinion on one power or the other and the character or intention of the disagreeing person must assign to the bishop or to the civil magistrate the trial and sentence of such cases. In both fields of belief and action merely to believe, either against the opinion of the government or of orthodox religion, and not to commit acts which are harmful to one or to the other must never justify corporal punishment or other deprivations of personal liberty. "For if it be necessary for all men to subscribe to the present religion [or present government], by the same reason at another time a man may be bound to subscribe to the contradictory, and so to all religions [or governments] in the world" (p. 535). This division of the religious and secular disciplines Taylor had introduced as early as his dedicatory letter to Sir Christopher Hatton in the phrase "the common principles of christianity, and those . . . [axiomata] . . . [of] civil society" (p. 343).

Now he has been so resolute and forthright in his more general considerations of practice that it is time theory were put to the actual test. Fortunately most so-called troublemakers are of weak minds and consciences which must neither be coddled nor by forcible means brought to the obedience of civil law or church discipline. At this second half of the second large part of his discourse, Taylor must get down to real cases, and he chooses two segments of current religious opinion which differ from his own, two "which are most troublesome and most disliked" (p. 540) in England in 1646, namely, the Anabaptists and the Church of Rome. Again, these two sects had been introduced in the letter to Hatton: "It is a hard case that we should think all papists and anabaptists . . . to be fools and wicked persons: certainly among all these sects there are very many wise men and good men, as well as erring" (p. 345). That Taylor does not pick out the militant Independents and vocal Presbyterians may show that he is more philosophical or politically astute than vindictive. Without incurring the too great displeasure of his immediate audience, he can well include the political and religious party temporarily in power by what he has to say of the Calvinistic doctrines of original sin that support part of the sectarian argument against paedobaptism.

These two sects do not enter here, as Heber says they do, merely because they were the two "most obnoxious" (I, clxxix). A better historical and philosophical reason is that suggested in another context by H. R. McAdoo: "The verdict of the Anglican was that Roman infallibilism tyranizes over conscience by striking at liberty, and the Puritan over liberty by offending against reason."[4] Rhetorically, the Anabaptists and Roman Catholics become the best examples here because of the meaning and shape of Taylor's whole argument and because they furnish the best "proofs" (in the sense of tests) of his theory. They are examples of cognition and will, faith and charity, philosophy and conduct, means and ends, just limits and temper, *effects* in behavior of *causes* in belief.

With the Anabaptists he finds that the arguments for believers' baptism (in practice this means adults) are no stronger nor weaker than those for vicarious baptism (in practice infants only). Hence, insofar as the arguments do not lead to practices which are inconsistent with just public ends or directly lead to a life of impiety, they must be tolerated despite the fact that "we Anglicans" do not agree with them. The opposition's insistence on believers' baptism, however, has no connection with many of their practices which actually come under the heading of civil disobedience. These acts are to be condemned since they are induced neither by doctrine nor by the desire to lead holy lives, but merely to harass the civil authority. Wherever their practices conflict with the law, let the civil authorities take care of them; ecclesiastical authority should never punish those persons who are guilty of these acts. Thus the Anabaptists are to be tolerated or not by the social results of their belief or lack of belief.

Taylor then proceeds to test his theory of toleration for Roman Catholics by the opposite method. Possessing a firmer foundation of faith than that which underlies the Anabaptists' total rejection of vicarious baptism, the Roman Catholics must be judged by the inducements (i.e., causes) which lead to practices (i.e., effects) that are inconsistent with public good or individual piety. The articles of faith he singles out for criticism in the Roman church of his day he calls superstructures, badly built upon the creedal foundation and managed even worse (p. 593). In practice some of these beliefs, like the Jesuitical justification to "murder Protestant princes" (most Englishmen believed that Guy Fawkes and Ravaillac were put on by the Jesuits), are plain treason and must be suppressed. Other practices, like deathbed repentance (one of Taylor's favorite bêtes noirs, given his insistence on the long and prayerful road to true repentance),[5] can lead to an unholy life. The doctrine behind it may not destroy faith, but it allows a man to live the life of a rake and be sure of heaven in his last five minutes. Though Taylor could not anticipate the notorious case of Lord Rochester, he must certainly have been aware that this practice was as common in the Anglican fold as it was in the Roman Catholic.

Having examined generally certain Roman doctrines which, superimposed upon the creed by designs that may be nonreligious, actually lead to condemnable practice in civil and moral life, Taylor returns to wholly speculative considerations in order to test two Roman Catholic articles of belief by their inducements and by their results. One is prayers for the dead. No possibly evil design could lie behind this, but only charity; whether the grounds for it are true or false, we must tolerate it. And indeed, though outlawed for a time during the Reformation as "papistical," prayers for the dead are retained by the Anglican church. The other article is the Roman Catholic belief in the transubstantiation of the elements in the Holy Eucharist. The quarrel on this point between Roman Catholic and Protestant has been long and bitter, despite the fact that the article lies quite outside both the Apostles' and the Nicene Creed. Some Protestants, with an Old Testament bias, score the belief as idolatry in that it seems to them to raise the simple bread and wine into objects which in themselves are to be worshiped. The second commandment, however, cannot touch any individual who in the Roman Catholic rite is innocent of actual idolatry. Besides, to punish on this account would be acting under Moses', not Christ's, law. Both of these Roman Catholic "religious opinions," therefore, may or may not be true, they may or may not be superstructures built onto a once solid foundation of Christian faith, but as long as they do not destroy piety and still meet the just demands of public law and order, they shall be tolerated, and their holders never, under any circumstances, shall be punished corporally.

This is Taylor's argument for the toleration of differing religious opinions, the form of it being inseparable from its substance. In the first part he defines faith and heresy, then practical courses of action connected with right reason in "prophesying" from Biblical texts; in the second part he begins with less theoretical matters and concludes with even more practical ones. Because the whole dichotomy is again dichotomized, there is a kind of descent, as in Plato's twice-bisected line, from IDEAS to hypotheses, to things, to images. Taylor's pairs of universal terms are constantly opposed and more often conjoined than left disjunctive. Throughout, the grounds for both admission as well as inadmission to toleration are perfectly clear.

Soon after he published his book, Dr. Samuel Rutherford (1600–1661), a principal Scottish Presbyterian in the Westminster Assembly and head of St. Mary's College at the University of Edinburgh, became convinced that Taylor's Arminian and Royalist tenets would open the gates of licentiousness. As early as 1636, Rutherford had argued against Arminianism in *Exercitationes Apologeticae pro Divina Gratia* in his attack on the "six Aberdeen doctors" for arguing so stubbornly against Aberdeen's signing the Covenant. In 1647 he challenged Jeremy Taylor in *A Free Disputation against Pretended Liberty of Conscience, tending to resolve doubts moved by Mr. J. Goodwin, John Baptist, Dr. Jer. Taylor . . . and other authors contending for lawless liberty, or licentiousness.* Today Rutherford lives mainly in Milton's sonnet against the "new forcers of conscience."[6]

The Liberty of Prophesying is often set side by side with Chillingworth's *The Religion of Protestants* (1638), written in the same great liberal tradition. Between the publication dates of the two works the Anglican church had been completely overthrown, the king captured, Laud and Strafford executed, the Independents triumphing over the Presbyterians, and uneducated sects proliferating. S. R. Gardiner said (I think mistakenly) that three-fourths of *The Liberty of Prophesying* was written under Chillingworth's influence;[7] and there is a strong tradition that Chillingworth criticized Taylor at All Souls, Oxford, for not taking into sufficient account his opponents' arguments.[8] My study of Taylor's polemical career convinces me that he does, but his method is more discursive than that of the debater who enumerates his opponent's arguments one by one. Chillingworth's book is unreadable today for its crabbed point-by-point refutation. By comparison, Taylor's free-flowing discourse is as impressive in its form as it is in its substance. Stylistically it is great for the very reason Edmund Gosse condemned it when it was the fashion to pick out Jeremy Taylor's similes: "It is bare and a little dry in statement," Gosse wrote: ". . . it presents few passages which could be separated from their context, and exhibited as specimens of English."[9] In substance Chillingworth, who suffered more than Taylor did at the hands of his Cromwellian captors, concludes that we should all be "plain and honest Christians." Taylor, on the other hand, anticipates our century by his insistence upon pluralism and the kind of ecumenical dialogue which can bring about greater unity and a truer vision.

His persuasiveness in argument and charity in temper is shown again on the subject of pluralism in a sermon preached at Golden Grove soon after he published *The Liberty of Prophesying:*

> From every sect and community of Christians take anything that is good, that advances holy religion and the divine honour. For one hath a better government, a second a better confession, a third hath excellent spiritual arts for the conduct of souls, a fourth hath fewer errors. And by what instrument soever a holy life is advantaged, use that, though thou grindest thy spears and arrows at the forges of the Philistines, knowing thou hast no master but Christ, no religion but the Christian, no rule but the scriptures and the laws and right reason (IV, 607).

So, as religion in George Herbert's phrase was standing tiptoe ready to come to the American strand, Roger Williams, the founder of Rhode Island, said that *The Liberty of Prophesying* had "excellently asserted the toleration of different religions, yea, in a respect, that of the papists themselves, which is a new way of soul freedom, and yet is the old way of Christ Jesus." [10]

Imprisonment and the Argument for
Freedom from Original Sin (1655-58)

IV

Taylor had been forcefully evicted from his parish in Uppingham in 1644; then he had joined the Royalist troops in Wales
as chaplain and had "landed" at Golden Grove. But Golden
Grove could not have been perfectly peaceful. Of his ten-year
span at the Carbery estate (1645-55), the first two years were
taken up with the argument for *The Liberty of Prophesying*
and the last year or more with the even more controversial
Unum Necessarium (1655). In the years between Taylor must
have been subject to periodic visitations by Cromwell's men.
Otherwise he could not have said in 1660 that he had "suffered
the persecution of eighteen years" for the Church of England
(I, ci). The "peace" of Golden Grove was there by temporary
permit and on condition.

Yet Golden Grove did furnish him with the time and place
for the rigorous practice of devotion. In 1649 he published
The Great Exemplar, a series of meditations on the main events
in the life of Christ. This was followed by his most popular
books of devotion, *Holy Living* in 1650 and *Holy Dying* in
1651. Meanwhile he prepared for publication the sermons he
had been delivering in the little chapel of the Carbery family,
thinking more and more on the necessity of individual repentance. The deaths of his first wife, of the first Lady Carbery,
and of two of his own children, as well as the swift defeat of

all he had fought for in the Royalist and Anglican cause—these events were for him an Armageddon.

Instead of surrendering to intellectual and spiritual despair, however, early in the year of 1655, to a published manual of daily prayers, Taylor recklessly gave the title *Golden Grove*—a name bound to raise the ire of the party in power in view of their distrust of past compromises. What is more, Taylor flaunted the name of Earl of Carbery in the dedication, and affixed to the book a fiery preface against the Presbyterians. Taylor's state of mind emerges from part of the litany in this apparently innocent manual:

> Remember not, O Lord, how we have been full of envy and malice, anger and revenge, fierce and earnest in the purchases and vanities of the world, and lazy and dull, slow, and soon weary in the things of God, and of religion. . . . Remember not, O Lord, our uncharitable behaviour towards those with whom we have conversed, our jealousies and suspicions, our evil surmizing and evil reportings, the breach of our promises to men, and the breach of all our holy vows made to thee our God.

And yet in this book's preface he wrote:

> But now, instead of this excellency of condition and constitution of religion [the Anglican Church], the people are fallen under the harrows and saws of impertinent and ignorant preachers, who think all religion is a sermon, and all sermons ought to be libels against truth and old governors,—and expound chapters that the meaning may never be understood,—and pray, that they may be thought able to talk, but not to hold their peace,—casting not to obtain any thing but wealth and victory, power and plunder. And the people have reaped the fruits apt to grow upon such crabstocks: they grow idle and false, hypocrites and careless; they deny themselves nothing that is pleasant; they despise religion, forget government; and some never think of heaven; and they that do, think to go thither in such paths which all the ages of the church did give men warning of, lest they should, that way, go to the devil.

As if this were not enough to anger the Parliamentary government with whose permission he was allowed to stay at Golden Grove, at the end of the same year, 1655, Taylor published *Unum Necessarium*, with its famous chapter VI which launched him into his battle against the Calvinistic reprobationist interpretation of the doctrine of original sin. This led to his imprisonment.

The argument on original sin is heralded by a simple story from the Gospel of St. Luke (10:38 ff.) that has a domestic setting and rings with essential truth, a story he had already used effectively in *The Liberty of Prophesying*. It is the story of Mary and Martha and how Mary had chosen "the one thing needful" while her sister did the kitchen chores. What is that one thing needful, the *"unum necessarium"* of his title, except to listen to the words of the Master? And if we listen, what is the word we hear? In 1655 Taylor wagered his life on this answer: what Jesus says to all who listen is that He came into this world to save us from our sins; and in return He requires of us repentance. The Presbyterian party now in power emphasized original sin, the doctrine of reprobation, and limited atonement. Taylor's succinct reaction is: you cannot repent of a sin you have not committed; repent of your own, not Adam's.

The Doctrine of Repentance

Repentance is the most pervasive doctrine in the whole of Taylor's writings—polemical, devotional, homiletic, and casuistical. One reason for this is that he shared with many in the seventeenth century, which opened with Hamlet's "The time is out of joint," an eschatological feeling that the world is drawing towards its end. " 'Tis too late to be ambitious," sighed Dr. Thomas Browne. Upon the defeat of the Royalist and Anglican cause, Taylor sought to get back to first things, which is man's sin and the hope of redemption—like Isaiah, and John the Baptist, and Jesus of Nazareth in similar periods of decay. To Taylor this is eminently practical. Even in so divisive a period of time as that marked by civil war, repentance is something we can do immediately; it is the practice of a faith.

One way of convincing ourselves of the centrality of its doctrine and practice in Taylor is to look at the exhaustive seventy-six-page "Index of the Principal Matters Contained in the Works of Bishop Taylor" which Heber made for his edition in 1822. Here "Repentance" occupies more space than any other doctrine, pointing to no less than twenty-six sustained passages in nine of the original fifteen volumes. By comparison, "Reason," so important an ingredient of *The Liberty of Prophesying* and of the seventeenth-century Anglican apologetic, refers in the same index to passages in only three volumes.

In an equally useful index, Heber collected every Biblical verse quoted in Taylor's works, and one notes how many and how often Taylor invoked those texts which speak of repentance, contrition, confession, and restitution with the expectation of forgiveness. Five times he quotes the phrase (from Matt. 3:18 and Acts 26:20), "fruits meet for repentance." Again, five times he quotes from 2 Cor. 7:10—"For Godly sorrow worketh repentance to salvation." He derives his doctrine that repentance is "one-half of the Christian Gospel" (II, 351) from Heb. 6:1, wherein the author declares that salvation is to be gained both by works and by faith, "works" being repentance for one's sins. Finally, a key verse for Taylor, quoted seven times, is 1 John 1:9—"If we confess our sins, he is faithful and just to forgive us our sins, and to cleanse us from all unrighteousness," a promise difficult to reconcile with our being damned in Adam. No texts are quoted more often and labored over more carefully than these on repentance.

Statistics, however, fade as proof of centrality when we look at Taylor's actual works. At the crisis of his life he writes a whole volume called *Unum Necessarium, or The Doctrine and Practice of Repentance. Describing the Necessities and Measures of a Strict, a Holy, and a Christian Life, and Rescued from Popular Errors* (1655). The emblematic frontispiece by Lombart, who engraved the best portrait of Jeremy Taylor we possess, shows the "Good Shepherd" with a lamb across his shoulders. "When I had entered upon . . . [this book]," Taylor confesses, "I found it necessary to do it in order to more purposes, and in prosecution of the method of my other studies" (VII, 6). These obviously consisted of the long planned work on "cases of conscience," *Ductor Dubitantium* (1660). Taylor begins the dedication of *Unum Necessarium*, again, to the earl of Carbery, with this:

> The duty of repentance is of so great and universal concernment, a *catholicon* for the evils of the soul of every man, that if there be any particular in which it is worthy of the labours of the whole ecclesiastical calling to be "instant in season and out of season" [2 Tim. 4:2] it is in this duty, and therefore I hope I shall be excused if my Discourses of Repentance, like the duty itself, be perpetually increasing . . . (VII, 3).

Central to the doctrine of the book is the controversy in which he hazarded his entire career, so convinced was he of its relevance to repentance and the Christian life, that is, the controversy on original sin as *the* "popular error" of his title.

As the misfortunes of the war gathered about him it seems as though Taylor more and more drew hope from Lent, the season that, ending in the triumph of Easter, begins with the "set form" of Ash Wednesday's collect:

> Almighty and everlasting God, who hatest nothing that thou hast made, and dost forgive the sins of all those who are penitent: Create and make in us new and contrite hearts, that we, worthily lamenting our sins and acknowledging our wretchedness, may obtain of thee, the God of all mercy, perfect remission and forgiveness; through Jesus Christ our Lord. Amen.

No more than a Christian should worship merely on Sundays and forget God the rest of the week, should he attend to so crucial a business for only six weeks by giving up beer. "For repentance," Taylor continues in the same dedication to Carbery, "is not like the summer fruits, fit to be taken a little and in their own time; it is like bread, the provision and support of our life, the entertainment of every day, but it is 'the bread of affliction' to some, and 'the bread of carefulness' to all; and he that preaches this with the greatest zeal and the greatest severity, it may be he takes the liberty of an enemy, but he gives the counsel and the assistance of a friend" (VII, 5).

To Jeremy Taylor, then, the way God works His "economy" is to give us a liberty of choice between good and evil; though a large part of our nature tempts us continually towards evil, another large part urges us as continually toward good. Knowing both sides of our nature, God cannot damn us eternally for the sins we commit if we are truly sorry for them and, confessing them, make known to Him our intention to lead a new life. How much less, given "the store-houses of heaven and the granaries of God" (lovely phrase from *Holy Living*), can the Great Economist damn us for the sins of Adam!

Instead of dismissing, with Coleridge and Heber, *Unum Necessarium* and its blast against the "popular" interpretation of original sin as an unfortunate theological and political aberration, therefore, we must take it as the climactic document in Taylor's career as Civil War controversialist. "The one thing necessary" in his religious economy is repentance for actual sins; if Calvinistic "original sin" stands in the way of true repentance, as Taylor was convinced it does, he must set out boldly to destroy the doctrine so that we can help God go about His real business here on earth.

Chepstow Prison

It was probably on direct order from Cromwell that Jeremy Taylor was arrested on his way back from London to Golden Grove in the spring of 1655 and imprisoned in Chepstow Castle. This ancient fortress in southern Wales was owned at the beginning of the Civil War by the Marquis of Worcester; it is just eight miles down the River Wye from Tintern Abbey. "The shores of the Wye are bold, rocky and woody," an eighteenth-century tourist wrote, "but the capital object which catches the eye, on the approach to Chepstow, is the castle, founded on a high, perpendicular cliff, rising from the river, and extended along its edge."[1] The castle was strategic to both parties, and the authority of the king or of Parliament prevailed in the west as either of them possessed it. Garrisoned by the Royalists under Colonel Fitzmorris, it fell easily in October, 1645, to Colonel (later Sir) Thomas Morgan at the head of three hundred horse and four hundred foot of Cromwell's army. It was recaptured for the king by Sir Nicholas Kemey, one of whose men swam across the river by stealth and entered the western gate. In an effort to regain it, Cromwell himself led a charge against the castle but without success, though it was defended by only one hundred and sixty Royalist troops. Cromwell left Colonel Isaac Ewer in command of a siege, and the Parliamentary forces finally won back Chepstow Castle on May 25, 1648, killing Colonel Kemey and forty of his men.

In recognition of his services to the state, Parliament settled the castle and the lands surrounding it upon Cromwell, who is paraphrased as having said, during the conference of November 25, 1654, on the retrenchment of army expenses, ". . . for Chepstow, because it was his own house, he would not have a garrison there at the Parliament's charge."[2] By Taylor's own word, he was treated at Chepstow not as a prisoner of a hardfisted garrison but as a gentleman guest. As such, he must have occupied a suite of three rooms in the southeastern round tower, later called Harry Marten's Tower for the famous regicide whom Charles the Second kept a prisoner there for twenty years until the man's death. From here Taylor carried on his argument on original sin which he had begun with the publication of *Unum Necessarium* from Golden Grove a few months before.

The exact time and extent of his imprisonment can be reasonably established. In the mid-1650's Cromwell was forced to treat the Anglicans with greater asperity. On Ash Wednesday of 1654 (February 8), Evelyn writes in his *Diary:* "In contradiction to all costome and decency, the usurper Cromwell

feasted at the Lord Maior's, riding in triumph thro' the Citty."[3]
On the following April 15 (1654) Evelyn heard "the famous
Dr. Jeremy Taylor" preach at St. Gregory's church near St.
Paul's from Matt. 6:48 on "evangelical perfection."[4]

Seven months later Evelyn writes to Taylor, evidently in
Wales, on February 9, 1655:

> I haue perused that excellent *Unum necessarium* of yours
> to my very greate satisfaction and direction: and do not
> doubt but it shall in tyme gaine upon all those exceptions,
> which I know you are not ignorant appeare against it.
> 'Tis a great deale of courage, and a greate deale of perill,
> but to attempt the assault of an errour so inveterate.[5]

The "errour so inveterate" is the Calvinist interpretation of
original sin which Taylor had attacked in chapter VI of the
first edition of *Unum Necessarium*.

Next month, on March 18, 1655, Evelyn goes to London
from his home at Sayes Court "on purpose to hear that excellent preacher Dr. Jeremy Taylor" on "the conditions of obtain-
ing eternal life."[6] At the end of this month, on March 31, 1655,
he visits Taylor to ask him to become his personal spiritual
adviser.[7] On April 8, 1655, apparently having discussed matters
of conscience with the great man, Evelyn heard Taylor preach
on Ps. 51:17—"The sacrifices of God are a broken spirit: a
broken and contrite heart, O God, thou wilt not despise."
Taylor must have been full of his subject, for Evelyn notes that
this sermon touched on "the degrees of Penitentiary Sorrow:
that no remanent affection to sin [is] consistent with true repentance."

At this point, while it is obvious from these sermons
preached to beleaguered Anglicans in London and from Evelyn's notes that the two had been thinking deeply for some time
on repentance, Taylor must have returned to Wales and was
captured, for eleven months now elapse before Evelyn records
seeing again his carefully chosen spiritual adviser. Taylor's imprisonment at Chepstow, therefore, must have begun in late
April or early May, 1655.

How long he was kept in prison is partly shown by the delay which he complains of in receiving letters. In answering Bishop Warner's first scolding for his views on original sin in chapter VI of *Unum Necessarium*, Taylor says:

> Your lordship's letter, dated July 28 [1655], I received not till September 11; it seems R. Royston detained it in his hands, supposing it could not come safely to me while I remain a prisoner now in Chepstow castle. But I now have that liberty that I can receive any letters, and send any; for the gentlemen under whose custody I am, as they are careful of their charges, so they are civil to my person (p. 541).

That he was there in September, 1655, is corroborated by Henry Hammond's letter to Gilbert Sheldon of September 14, 1655, which, incidentally, witnesses once again to the Anglican perturbations Taylor's stand on original sin caused: "Dr. Taylor's book is matter of much discourse, and in that point of Orig. Sinn disliked by everyone. . . . I wish with you hee would advise before hee runs these hazards. But I feare, it will not bee. Poor man hee is in affliction at Cheepstow castle."[8] Bishop Warner's more scathing letter, we learn from Taylor, was dated November 10 [1655], and Taylor apparently answers it from prison (p. 560).

His imprisonment also coincides with Cromwell's increasingly severe proclamations aimed at the Anglicans. The decree of November 1, 1655, provided that none of the Royalist party were to keep in their houses chaplains, ejected ministers, or college fellows; or keep school, teach children, administer sacraments, or use *The Book of Common Prayer*, on pain of three months' imprisonment for the first offense, six months', for the second, and banishment, for the third.[9] Taylor had been notoriously guilty of every one of these particulars both at Golden Grove and in London. Cromwell's edict forbidding public Anglican worship was published on November 27, 1655. On Christmas Day, 1655, Evelyn records hearing Dr. Wild preach from 2 Cor. 13:9

the funeral sermon of Preaching, this being the last day, after which Cromwell's proclamation was to take place, that none of the Church of England should dare either to preach or administer Sacraments, teach schools, &c. on paine of imprisonment or exile. So this was ye mournfullest day that in my life I had seene, or ye Church of England herselfe, since ye Reformation; to the greate rejoicing of both Papist and Presbyter.[10]

The duration of Taylor's imprisonment at Chepstow is also shown by the amount of work which he accomplished while there. A man of his stature in learning and piety most probably served the garrison and inmates as chaplain and preacher. And though he was a swift and prolific writer, here he wrote the extra chapter of *Unum Necessarium* with a great deal more on original sin, carried on his controversy with the Anglican bishops and others, wrote *Deus Justificatus* on the same subject, and within only one year, that is on March 25, 1657, showed Evelyn the manuscript of his long incubated *Ductor Dubitantium* ready for the press, much of which must have been written while he was in prison.[11]

Finally, indications of just when he was released from Chepstow are given to us once more by his friend Evelyn. In a letter to Taylor dated "Mar. 18, 1655" but which must be in our reckoning 1656, Evelyn expresses great relief that Taylor is out of danger; he also speaks passionately of the effects of Cromwell's edict forbidding public worship by Anglicans: "Julianus Redivivus can shut the schooles indeed and the temples; but he cannot hinder our private intercourses and devotions, where the breast is the chappell and our heart is the altar."[12] In this letter Evelyn continues with a reference to Taylor's further writings on original sin since the publication of *Unum Necessarium:*

Sr, I have not yet been so happy as to see those papers, which Mr. Royston tells me are printing, but I greatly rejoice that you haue so happily fortified that batterie; and I doubt not but you will maintaine the seige: for you must

not be discouraged for the passions of a few. Reason is
reason to me where euer I find it, much more where it con-
duces to a designe so salutary and necessary. At least, I
wonder that those who are not convinced by yr arguments, can possibly resist yr charity, and yr modesty. . . .
I am confident tyme will render you many more proselytes.

In what must be the response to this letter from Evelyn,
Jeremy Taylor writes: "Not long after my comming from my
prison (Chepstow) I mett with your kind and freindly letters.
. . ." Taylor is happy for Evelyn's progress in piety, which
Evelyn in the March 18 letter had just described. In a new
paragraph Taylor then responds to his friend's reference to the
controversy on original sin:

> I am well pleased that you haue read over my last
> booke; and give God thankes that I have reason to beleive
> that it is accepted by God, and by some good men. As for
> the censure of unconsenting persons, I expected it, and
> hope that themselves will be their owne reproovers; and
> truth will be assisted by God, and shall prevaile, when all
> noises and prejudices shall be ashamed. My comfort is, that
> I have the honour to be the advocate for God's justice and
> goodnesse, and that the consequent of my doctrine is that
> men may speake honour of God and meanly of themselves.
> But I have also this last weeke sent up some papers in
> which I make it appeare that the doctrine which I now
> haue published was taught by the fathers within the first
> 400 years; and haue vindicated it both from novelty and
> singularity. I have also prepared some other papers con-
> cerning this question, which I once had some thoughts to
> have published. But what I have already said, and further
> explicated and justified, I hope may be sufficient to satisfy
> pious and prudent persons, who doe not love to goe *qua
> itur* but *qua eundum est*. Sr, you see what a good husband
> I am of my paper and inke, that I make so short returnes
> to your most friendly letters.[13]

This epistolary exchange accomplished, after an absence
from Evelyn's house of eleven months, Taylor returns, for on

April 12, 1656, Evelyn records that he dined at Sayes Court, the other guests being Robert Boyle and Wilkins.[14] Four days later Taylor sends Evelyn a thank-you note.[15] On May 6, 1656, Evelyn introduces him to a young Sorbonnist, Monsieur J. le Franc, for nomination for orders in the Anglican church, and the young French theologian and Jeremy Taylor discuss in Latin the doctrine of original sin.[16]

Thus from Evelyn's *Diary* and correspondence, from Cromwell's proclamations ending Anglican activity in London, and from Taylor's own writings in Chepstow, it may be safely deduced that he was a prisoner there for ten months, from late April or early May, 1655, to March, 1656.

While a prisoner in Chepstow Castle he determined to drive his controversial interpretation of original sin "on to the utmost issue." Its initial blast had already shocked some ruling members of his own church anxious to keep what little remained of it. When the Calvinistic-Presbyterian party was ruling England, Taylor dared in the name of freedom to challenge even the victors on so central a theological and political issue as that of "unconditional election." Evelyn had supported him by calling their doctrine an "inveterate error." It is an error to Taylor because it invalidates repentance. And that it is inveterate Taylor knew from reading its history.

A Brief History of the Concept of Original Sin[17]

The doctrine of original sin must begin with man's first consciousness of evil in the world. Why is it that most men know that love, and wisdom, and justice are palpable goods experientially arrived at, yet rule their lives and the lives of others by hate, stupidity, and extortion? Greek tragedy, especially that of Aeschylus, broods on this dark theme.

For the Hebraic-Christian view of life, the existential fact of sin is given mythically in Genesis, chapters 3–4, in the story of Adam and Eve and the murder of their son Abel by his own brother Cain. Christian theologians early found here hints of either a total depravity or else an imputation of guilt that connects Adam's sin to his descendants' liability to punishment. Also Ps. 51:5—"Behold, I was shapen in iniquity; and in sin did my mother conceive me"—seemed to some later Christians to make us congenitally sinful. Yet as the concept developed in Jewish thought, the individual alone is responsible for giving in to his own evil imagination: for example, Ezek. 18:4—"Behold, all souls are mine: as the soul of the father, so also the soul of the son is mine: the soul that sinneth, it shall die."

Jesus does not mention original sin, though in everything He said sin may be implicit in the emphasis upon the necessity for redemption. In the New Testament St. Paul first gives it extended treatment, but St. Paul's ideas in Romans, the *locus classicus* for Christians who worry about it, have subsequently accommodated innumerable and conflicting theories. What is the mediating link between Adam's sin and death in us? Seminal existence as it is hinted in Heb. 7:9 ff. ? In Romans, does Paul refer our sin to Adam's in the sense that Christians die to sin as they believe Christ died on the cross—that is, merely in a metaphorical or typological sense? All we can be sure of is that in the almost endless commentaries on Romans throughout the history of Christian thinking, nothing emerges from Paul's often metaphorical language except that many have taken some figures of speech (such as that of the potter and the pots) literally.

Starting from the Jewish and Pauline doctrines, the early church fathers divided into what might be called the "hard" and the "soft" schools. Origen, for example, began by treating the Genesis narrative as allegory intending all souls in a Phaedrus-like preexistence, so that original sin is derived not from Adam but from each person's individual will. But he changed this when he came across infant baptism after he had been banished from Alexandria for so "soft" a theory; he decided that baptism in infants, which he saw in Caesarea, existed to wash away the stain of sin which a baby must have inherited from Adam's corruption. A more dangerously "soft" father was the second century Tatian, in whose *Apology* first appears the concept of "original righteousness," later taken up by Duns Scotus. "Original sin" becomes, then, merely the deprivation of the supernatural gift of grace enjoyed by prelapsarian man, and not the cause, from Adam's disobedience, of an irrevocably dislocated human nature.

The necessity to confute the Pelagian heresy turned St. Augustine into the "hardest" church father on the subject of original sin. Where orthodox Christianity depends on synergism, or the dualistic thrust of both God ("down to man", so to speak) and of man ("up to God", so to speak), Pelagius and his followers set man up so high as to make God almost unnecessary. To prove how incapable man is by himself, Augustine, particularly in *De Peccato Originali*, had to prove that man is born a sinner as he is born in Adam, a theory that adumbrates the total depravity spoken of by John Calvin.

In the Middle Ages the "hard" and the "soft" schools became extremes, with St. Thomas Aquinas as moderating middle. Peter Lombard carried on the tradition of Augustinian depravity. Against this stood Anselm, followed by Occam and Scotus. Scotus believed that Adam's sin was not an incomprehensible defiance of his Creator but the natural and pardonable defect of love for Eve. Sex, in other words, which so unfortunately for the whole discussion gets wound up in it, is a morally neutral physical appetite built into man by God Himself. Between Lombard's Augustinian depravity and the amelioration of Duns Scotus stood Aquinas. Denying that natural goodness was forfeited at the Fall, he insisted that free will was only impaired, not inexorably taken away; for Aquinas, man is a born sinner who is free to choose eternal damnation or salvation, with a predilection for the former.

At the Council of Trent (1545–63), the two medieval extremes in the views of original sin were represented by the Jesuits and the Dominicans. There, the Jesuits, favoring Dun Scotus's "soft" theory, argued that Adam fell from a supernature to a nature. The Dominicans, on the other hand, took the "hard" view of St. Augustine that Adam fell from nature to a subnature. One reason for calling the Council of Trent was to resist Calvin's *Institutes* (1535). Thousands were being drawn away by it from the moderate Catholic position toward Calvin's "five points": total depravity, unconditional election, limited atonement, irresistible Grace, and the perseverance of the saints. In its insistence on the almost single thrust of God (man practically incapable of exerting any thrust at all), strict Calvinism is as antisynergistic in one direction as Pelagianism is in the other. The Council of Trent, therefore, adopted the middle position of Aquinas between the Jesuitical and Dominican extremes.

When the Marian Protestant exiles began to return to England at the accession of Edward VI to the throne, they brought with them a theology deeply imbued with Calvinism. Pressure was brought upon Archbishop Cranmer to make his 1553 "Articles" on the subject of original sin almost as "hard" as St. Augustine's. The Tridentine Articles, as we have seen, were Thomistically moderate. Though Cranmer himself may have been more sympathetic with the Lutheran emphasis upon the "Grace of God," he was practically forced to differ as much as possible from the adopted Roman view, and consequently to emphasize with the Calvinists the "sovereignty of God." To John Calvin on March 20, 1552, Cranmer wrote: "Our adversaries now hold a council at Trent, endeavouring to establish errors, and shall we neglect to hold a godly synod, in which we may refute errors, correct erroneous doctrines, and set forth those things which are true?"[18] At that time the English church could be a "reformed" church only by being anti-Catholic and declaring for original sin in its Augustinian rather than in its Thomistic frame.

At the Council of Dort (1617–18), the "soft" pleas of the Remonstrants for that kind of *recta ratio* which underlies Hooker's Anglicanism fell before the "hard" arguments used by the theologians from Geneva, sent to Dortrecht in Holland for the great debate. The English observers represented rather King James than the English church, since as a Scottish theologian himself James sided with the Calvin-Knox thinking of Fran. Gomarus (1563–1641), the Dutch theologian who opposed the liberal Remonstrants.[19] Two of James's observers certainly held Calvinistic views on predestination, Joseph Hall, later bishop of Norwich, and Dr. John Davenant, professor of theology at Cambridge. And though the mild John Hales of Eton said good-night to Calvin "at the well pressing of Episcopius of John 3: 16," he never said good-morning to the Remonstrants.[20] Led by Episcopius and Hugo Grotius, the anti-Calvin forces at Dort had prepared their arguments (in vain, it turned out) from such "soft" thinkers on original sin as Castellio and Arminius.

Sebastian Castellio (1515–63) became famous for his four posthumously published dialogues (1578): *De Praedestinatione, De Electione, De Libero Arbitrio,* and *De Fido,* which became four of the five points in Arminius's arguments *contra* Calvin.[21] Castellio asserted that the prophets of Israel made up the fiction of Adam's sin, and then, to explain the destruction of Sodom and Gomorrah, invented the doctrine that God is just and that nothing can come about except through His will. Castellio sought to deny Calvin's Augustinian premises on grounds of Biblical exegesis and human psychology.[22] Believing that Christianity is a religion not of despair and death but of hope and life, Castellio has his two fictional disputants, Ludovicus and Fredericus, argue the points back and forth in the form of a Platonic dialogue. The negative thrust is the refutation of Calvin's central doctrines; the positive, Castellio's consistent emphasis upon justification by faith. Here one of his favorite emblems is that of the fallen tree newly grafted by Christ, symbolizing the universality of Grace offered gratuitously by God through His son to all for all eternity.

Arminius (1560–1609), despite the fact that he had died before the Council of Dort was called, was the other leading liberal thinker in its deliberations. Basing his theology on the Bible, of course, and its patristic interpreters, Arminius was the most outspoken critic of Calvinistic doctrine: "I reject this Predestination," he says, "(1) because it is not the foundation of Christianity—'he that believeth shall be saved' is; (2) because it comprises neither the whole nor any part of the Gospel; (3) because it was never admitted as orthodox by any council in the first six centuries of the Christian era; [and] (4) because it

71

is repugnant to the nature of God and opposed to the nature of man."[23] Even more specifically, in his letter to Junius, Arminius argues against the views of Calvin and of Beza together, of St. Thomas, and of St. Augustine, since all of them agree that "God, by an eternal and immutable decree, determined to bestow upon certain men, the rest being passed by, supernatural and eternal life, and those means which are the necessary and efficacious prepositions for the attainment of that life."[24]

The view of Calvin that God pre-elects or pre-reprobates men not yet created, Arminius argues, makes God the author of sin by allowing some men to fall in order that He can save others. To Aquinas's middle view that God creates men in a natural state and then leaves them in that state or raises them from it, Arminius says, ". . . no man was ever created by God in merely a natural state"[25] since the grace of God is evangelical, not legal. Finally, against St. Augustine, Arminius added further arguments in his review in 1602 of William Perkins's *Treatise Concerning the Order and Mode of Predestination.*[26] Arminius cannot believe that God allows some to lie in a lump of perdition (a reference to the potters and the pots of Romans, chapter 9) to show His justice, and delivers others from that damnation to show His mercy. The passage by St. Paul on the "vessels of wrath" and the "vessels of mercy" is an analogy, Arminius argues, not to be taken literally: the difference between a clay pot and a man is that a man has free will.[27]

Such anti-Calvinistic ideas as these were wittily expressed by "O.N." in a dialogue entitled *An Apology of English Arminianism* (Oxford, 1634). "The Authour whereof," he writes in the preface, "supposeth Arminius to be living at this present, and to have read all such Bookes of Protestants, as have been written, touching the Questions heere disputed of. All which liberty the Nature of a Dialogue permitteth to any Writer."[28] So he imagines "Enthusiastus" and his Calvinistic friends at The Hague debating with Arminius in Leyden, but they are roundly beaten on such propositions as (1) man's will is free, (2) no man is infallibly assured of his salvation, (3) justifying faith may not be lost, and (4) God does not reprobate any man to damnation without reference to his wicked works. The same Arminian tenet of free will emerges poetically in Milton's *Paradise Lost:*

> And I will place within them as a guide
> My umpire Conscience, whom if they will hear,
> Light after light well us'd they shall attain,
> And to the end persisting, safe arrive (III, 194–97).

Upon such views as these of Castellio and Arminius the Remonstrants at Dort attempted to win the day, but they lost.[29] The Calvinist victory at Dort strengthened the English Presbyterians, Independents, and Geneva-inclined Anglicans, so that the rational Arminian voice of the Anglican church was hardly heard above the din of the Westminster Assembly, whose views on original sin now form the final chapter in this brief history.

Taylor had already taken notice of its *Directory* in his initial argument for "considered" rather than extempore prayer. The fourth chapter of the 1645 *Directory for the Publique Worship of God*, entitled "Of the Fall of Man, and of Sin, and the Punishment thereof," is so important to Taylor's final controversy that it must be quoted in full:

> I. Our first Parents being seduced by the subtilty, and temptation of Satan sinned in eating the forbidden fruit. This their sin God was pleased according to his wise and holy counsell to permit, having purpose to his own glory [Romans 14:32]
>
> II. By this sin they fell from their original righteousness and communication with God, and so became dead in sin, and wholly defiled in . . . their soul and body
>
> III. They being the root of all mankind, the guilt of this sin was imputed, and the same death in sin and corrupted nature conveyed to all their posterity descended from them by ordinary generation
>
> IV. From this original corruption, whereby we are utterly indisposed, disabled, and made opposite to all good, and wholly inclined to evil, do proceed all actual transgressions

V. This corruption of nature during this life, doth remain in those that are regenerated, and although it be, through Christ, pardoned and mortified, yet both it self and all the motions thereof are truly and properly sin

VI. Every sinne, both originall and actuall, being a transgression of the righteous Law of God, and contrary thereunto, doth in its own nature bring guilt upon the sinner, whereby he is bound over to the wrath of God, and curse of the Law, and so made subject to death, with all miseries, spirituall [Eph. 4:7], temporall [Rom. 8:20], and eternal [2 Thess. 1:9].[30]

Besides this chapter on original sin, other parts of the *Directory for the Publique Worship* were certain to have caught Taylor's attention, for example, chapter X—"Of effectual calling":

All those whom God hath predestinated unto life, and those only, he is pleased in his appointed and accepted time, effectually to call, by his Word and Spirit, out of that state of sin and death, in which they are by nature, to grace and salvation by Jesus Christ. . . . Elect infants dying in infancy are regenerated and saved by Christ through the Spirit. . . . Others not elected [i.e., infants and adults] although they may be called by the Ministry of the Word, and may have some common operations of the Spirit, yet they never truely come unto Christ, and therefore cannot be saved.[31]

The "Larger Catechism" in this book, "agreed upon by the Assembly of Divines at Westminister," typically runs like this:

Q. *Wherein* consisteth the sinfullnesse of this *estate whereunto man fell? A* . . . . in the guilt of *Adams* first sinne, the want of that righteousness wherein he was created, and the corruption of his nature whereby he is utterly indisposed, disabled, and made opposit unto all that is spiritually good, and wholly inclined to evil, and that continually, which is commonly called Originall Sin, and from which do proceed all actuall transgressions.[32]

Acting as first prolocutor of the Westminster Assembly, the Reverend William Twisse (1578?–1646) arrayed himself against such Anglicans as Dean Thomas Jackson of Peterborough, Dr. John Goodwin of Coleman Street, Laud's personal envoy Dr. Samuel Hoard, and Canon Christopher Potter of Windsor. Like Taylor, Potter, fruitlessly it seems, refused to be called names: "I resolve never to be an Arminian," he cried, "and ever to be a moderate. . . . Reason shall drive me from any opinion (for I will espouse none out of obstinacy) and Truth ever command me."[33] Dr. Twisse, however, was adamant in his reprobationist views, and against Samuel Hoard wrote *The Riches of God's Love unto the Vessels of Mercy consistent with His Absolute Hatred or Reprobation of the Vessels of Wrath; or An Answer unto a book entitled God's Love unto Mankind, Manifested by Disproving His Absolute Decree for Their Damnation* (Oxford, 1653). The title page quotes Rom. 9:20–21 on the potter and the pots, and the book asserts from texts that reprobation is right both in its sublapsarian and supralapsarian forms. God is not blamed for man's destruction, Twisse argues, since reprobation still recognizes man's sin for man's sin; reprobation does not deprive us of conscience, nor the feeling of guilt; and reprobation is not fatalism and not contrary to Scripture or to God's holiness, mercy, and justice.[34]

In view of Taylor's denial of each one of these propositions, it is significant that to this book by Twisse there are two commendatory letters from the Reverend Henry Jeanes of Chedzoy, Somersetshire, who at the end of the book undertakes to refute John Goodwin's refutation of Twisse's argument. In his letter, Jeanes writes: "If any Armenian [*sic*] whatsoever will give a Just, Full, and Scholasticall Answer unto It, I shall by God's helpe returne him a reply; for 'tis De Causa Dei (as Bradwardine Entitles his Booke), and in defence of

God's Cause I shall feare no Colours."[35] True to his word, he entered the lists against Jeremy Taylor in 1657.

Taylor's Argument

Taylor's argument went far beyond a revulsion against the doctrine of reprobation; it was the inevitable challenge to his own "liberty of prophesying." First came *Unum Necessarium* with its famous chapter VI, "On Original Sin." Taylor had already corresponded about this chapter with Bishops Brian Duppa and John Warner and knew that the chapter would offend. When he published the book, he placed before it a "Preface to the Right Reverend and Religious Fathers, Brian Lord Bishop of Sarum, and John Lord Bishop of Rochester, and to the Most Reverend and Religious Clergy of England, my dear Brethren." Imagine the shock these two bishops suffered at seeing their names before such a doctrine as the book contained. Taylor wrote another short piece, "A Further Explication of the Doctrine of Original Sin," which in subsequent editions became chapter VII, following the original chapter VI. The two bishops had remonstrated on different grounds. Duppa was afraid of the times; publishing such a chapter at that time would be very inexpedient. To Taylor this was timid but possibly wise. Bishop Warner, however, argued vehemently in a letter that Taylor was just not true; this deserved a different answer, the extra chapter and a letter to Warner. The bishop of Rochester replied in a letter dated July 11, 1655, received by Taylor in Chepstow prison, and so acknowledged. Though Warner's letter is not extant, we can reconstruct it from Taylor's point by point refutation. Warner replied to Taylor's reply on November 10, 1655, and in return got another reply from Taylor. Meanwhile Taylor had written to the Countess of Devonshire a clear account of his position on the problem, which was published by Royston in 1656 without the author's permission, as *Deus Justificatus, or a vindication of the glory of the divine attributes in the question of original sin; against the*

76

presbyterian way of understanding it. Taylor acknowledged the anonymous pamphlet as his own and republished it with Royston the following year, suppressing only the name of the original recipient and substituting for it "written to a person of quality." This was the last of his many formal words on the subject, but he was far from through. Dr. Jeanes of Chedzoy had attacked him in 1657 (as he had earlier promised to challenge an "Arminian" who dared oppose Dr. Twisse), and in 1660 published without permission his and Taylor's exchange. With the return of Charles II and the reestablishment of the Anglican church, Taylor had earned—through his piety, loyalty, and erudition—a bishopric. He was assigned a "safe" one in northern Ireland, where he had found temporary refuge in 1658 in Lord Conway's household near Lisburn.

The controversy on original sin, then, was actually the climax of Taylor's life. Begun and ended for reasons of piety and conducted throughout with skill and urgency, it brought together Taylor's whole lifework from the early argument in favor of liturgy to his final book on cases of conscience. And had he not fought it, that phrase of his which Logan Pearsall Smith applied to him would not sound quite so lonely: "a divine who once wore a mitre, and is now a little heap of dust."[36]

We have seen that *The Liberty of Prophesying* is a single, sustained argument as important in its shape as in its doctrine. The present argument, however, is scattered through a dozen documents over a period of three years. It is filled with repetitions, backtracking, windings, and rare bursts of temper at people who could not understand that his purpose throughout was "the necessity for repentance." Rather than treat this controversy, therefore, as we treated *The Liberty of Prophesying*, we shall have to take an overview.

To begin with, the grounds are the same, and the usual grounds of the Anglican apologist: Scripture, tradition, and reason, with reason applied to the interpretation of the Bible and to the meaning of history. At the end of the extra chapter of *Unum Necessarium* (which became chapter VII in subsequent editions), Taylor writes: "I hope I have done my duty, having produced scripture, and reasons, and the best authority" (VII, 340).[37] Again, as is usual in seventeenth-century Anglican argumentation, reason does not intend the close syllogistic brand of Aristotle and St. Thomas, but a scepticism, a weighing of alternatives in the scale of common sense, a trust in the "more probable," and an appeal to most right-thinking men in a "Platonic" not-only-but-also dialectic. Right reason is intelligence augmented by ethics, religion, and good sense. Thus Taylor declares his grounds to be "Scripture and right reason, and the doctrine of the primitive church for the first three hundred years" (p. 19). To Bishop Warner he asserts: "In this I have not only scripture and all the reason of the world on my side, but the complying sentences of the most eminent writers of the primitive church" (p. 565). Since part of his argument must be against Article IX of the Anglican "Thirty-nine Articles," he examines his case "according to scripture and right reason" only since the Articles are not part of the best tradition. Reexamining St. Paul's theories of original sin, he proposes to "separate the certain from the uncertain, that which is revealed from that which is presumed, that which is reasonable from that which makes too bold reflections upon God's honour, and the reputation of His justice and His goodness" (p. 244). For example, Taylor wonders why Calvinists insist on "difficult" and "obscure" passages in St. Paul to "prove" determinism and overlook so clear a statement on freedom as 1 Cor. 7:37: "He that standeth steadfast in his heart, having no necessity, but hath power over his own will, and hath so decreed in his heart . . . [he] doeth well." Thus the three grounds of right reason, the Bible, and the authority of history overlap and intertwine, sometimes one ground emerging as more important, sometimes another, but still standing firm as the court of every appeal.

On these grounds Taylor erects his argument against the then usual view of damnation for original sin. Professor D. P. Walker has recently traced in the history of Christian thought how the harrowing of hell and the concept of reprobation have undergone a mitigation.[38] Taylor is important, among other things, for anticipating many twentieth-century views. It is well known that both the Presbyterians in the seventeenth century and a large segment of the Anglican church inherited Calvin; also that today's average Presbyterian has come a long way from Calvinistic concepts of election and reprobation. To paraphrase Milton, Taylor might have said, "Your Anglican bishop is but your Presbyter writ large." But for controverting the doctrines then held of original sin he was called "Papist," "Socinian," and "Pelagian," and found himself attacked by Presbyterians and not surprisingly by his own church. Charles II was advised to keep this dangerous liberal in Ireland.

Throughout the battle Taylor used three main arguments: the argument of truth, the argument of ethics, and the argument of religion. In the first, being a learned man, he is not interested in mere custom but in actual truth (if he can find it) of Biblical interpretation, history, and human psychology. In the second, being a practical man, he fights for those views on the problem of original sin which make individual men better and societies peaceful. In the third, being a pious and devoted Christian, he speaks for those views which add to the greater glory of God. He is satisfied that he has made a contribution to religious knowledge (p. 339). The usual doctrines of original sin, he asserts, are false, inimical to good behavior, and dishonorable to God's goodness and justice. In other words they are contrary to truth as we can find the truth, to man's best interests, and to God Himself. Taylor's views, on the contrary, would have to be true, workable, and holy; so that his three arguments become *cognoscenda*, *agenda*, and *credenda*. Here again is an interesting parallel with his great contemporary, Milton, for these exactly coincide with the three criteria for knowledge which Raphael sets for his inquisitive student Adam in the Garden of Eden. Adam can know those things which (1) are within his capacity to know—"what thou canst attain"; (2) "infer thee also happier"; and (3) "best may serve to glorify the Maker" (*P.L.*, VII, 115–20).

I

Certainly the first problem must be the "truth" of Adam's fall. Is it true that we inherit that "original" sin and thus are guilty of it? St. Paul, St. Augustine, John Calvin, and innumerable other commentators have had their say about it. *Katachrestikos* is the word that intends Adam's sin, the first disobedience in the great Hebrew myth, and he was punished for it. Punishment is usually thought of as a deprivation of something which the sinning person once possessed. The truth of the story in Genesis, Taylor believes, is that Adam at creation had a natural grace, a *superadditum* which God justly took away from him as punishment. This is what God threatened and nothing more. As a result natural man (and we inherit Adam's nature) cannot by his own strength arrive at a supernatural end; so that grace, after the fall, became a free gift. All that the Bible tells us clearly is that we have received more by the "second Adam," Christ, than we lost by the first. In view of the charges hurled at Taylor of Pelagianism, it must be clear that where the Pelagians asserted that Adam's fall does not involve mankind, Taylor insists that it does. Among his many statements to this effect, we need quote only one now, at the beginning of *Deus Justificatus:* "But first, . . . be pleased to remember that the question is not whether there by any such thing as original sin; for it is certain and confessed on all hands almost. For my part, I cannot but confess that to be which I feel, and groan under, and by which all the world is miserable" (VII, 497). And where the Pelagians were "heretical" in arguing that man is capable of perfection without divine grace, Taylor consistently argues that in God's economy our necessary dependence upon grace was purchased for us by Adam's disobedience.[39]

And yet some of Taylor's opponents would say that it is as natural for fallen man to sin as it is for him to be hungry, and all this depends upon how one "prophesies" from Romans, chapters 5, 6, and 7. Surely sin entered by Adam, and surely death came upon all men between Adam and Moses from that root, Taylor would argue (Rom. 5:13-14). After the giving of

Moses' law, the sin which was in the world now became punishable in all who broke the law. Adam, therefore, was the cause of our death until Moses; after Moses, Adam is only the precedent. We ourselves are the cause of a decision to obey or disobey the Ten Commandments, and many men, knowing well the consequences, choose to disobey. With the coming of Christ a second choice was given: to repent or not to repent of one's sin. Taylor argues here by familiar seventeenth-century typology, Christ being the "second Adam."

This is how Taylor, along with many others, would interpret Rom. 12:19—"For as by one man's disobedience many were made sinners, so by the obedience of one shall many be made righteous." To his general interpretation, however, Taylor brings variant meanings of the term "sin" (p. 248). Sometimes, as in Heb. 9:28, "sin" means the punishment of sin. Again, as in Heb. 7:27, "sin" imputed to Christ must mean Christ's infirmity as the Son of man, that is, the condition of His mortal body. The condition of being mortal is concupiscence, but concupiscence is not a sin. It is only "the first motions and inclinations to sin" (p. 249), which were even in Adam. The question remains: what really was the effect of Adam's sin and what evil descended as a consequence upon us?

Adam, Taylor concludes, was created immortal. Forfeiting that gift, he was left in what Taylor calls his natural mortal state. His sin infected us with death, which we derive from our birth; that is, we too are born mortal and have to die. Even an infant, St. Cyprian says, who has had no chance to sin, is mortal; and infant mortality cannot possibly be punishment for Adam's sin. Mortality is a condition of being born, but God through Christ has given us an opportunity to escape even this "law." Adam's sin, then, hurts us, but it cannot damn us.

Let us invent a parable to illustrate Taylor's reasoning at this point. Suppose an American businessman, of good reputation in his community, is convicted of embezzlement, fined $10,000, and put into prison for ten years. As a result, his son, aged thirteen at the time, becomes emotionally disturbed and drops out of school. He is not being punished for his father's crime, nor has he committed a crime of his own. The condition of his life has only been made a lot harder for him because of what his father did. But by dint of that handicap he may succeed even more than his father, especially if a benefactor, perceiving the boy's misfortune and promise, volunteers to "adopt" him. In this way, Taylor would argue, we are all the "sons" of Adam and of Christ.

Original sin, according to the Calvinists, is a want of original righteousness, and, according to the Roman Catholics, concupiscence. Because the Church of England "hath not determined that either of them is formally a sin, or inherent in us, I may with the greater freedom," Taylor continues, "discourse concerning the several parts" (p. 310). And this brings him to the "truth" of Article IX of the Anglican church and the historical conditions that gave it birth. Since here Taylor argues against Calvinistic views of damnation which, in his mind, dishonor the wisdom and justice of God, we shall postpone it for the time being.

So much for the argument of truth, a truth secured to Taylor mainly by the principles enunciated in *The Liberty of Prophesying* to bring right reason to bear upon the interpretation of the Bible, particularly the fifth chapter of Romans, which gave rise to *one* of the Christian doctrines concerning original sin.

II

His next argument is an ethical one: those views of original sin are best which allow us to live better lives. "Sin" in its theological context causes us to do "evil" in a social context. Like Milton, Taylor clings to free will and the consequent centrality of choice in the ethical life. Adam's sin does not bind us to continual evil; to think thus is self-deception and worse, self-excuse. Eve blamed the serpent, Adam blamed Eve, we blame Adam, but each consciously chose evil rather than good, and faced with the consequence sought self-exculpation. "Thou art deceived," Taylor quotes Seneca as saying (p. 263), "if thou thinkest that vices are born with us; no, they are superinduced and come in upon us afterwards."

Yet many attempt to prove that we are congenitally evil by quoting Psalm 51:5—"Behold, I was shapen in iniquity; and in sin did my mother conceive me." Taylor deplores the anti-sexuality in the many interpretations of this verse from the time of St. Augustine to his own. To him sex is not sin and it is not evil: it may be part of the animality of man, but it is saved from carnality by love and marriage. David at that verse, Taylor believes, is being penitential, not self-exculpatory. "No man," he continues, "can perish for being an 'animal' man, that is for not having any supernatural revelations, but for not consenting to them when he hath, that is, for being 'carnal' as well as 'animal'; and that he is 'carnal' is wholly his own choice" (p. 269). Again, "A man is naturally inclined to desire the company of a woman whom he fancies," Taylor says. "This is naturally no sin: for the natural desire was put into us by God, and therefore could not be evil" (p. 277). Furthermore, inveterate Bible quoters take "shapen in iniquity" out of its Jewish context. It does not refer to original sin, for in the same Psalm appear, before this verse, "Wash me thoroughly from mine iniquity, and cleanse me from my sin; for I acknowledge my transgressions, and my sin is ever before me" (Ps. 51:2–3), and, after the verse, one of Taylor's favorites, "The sacrifices of God are a broken spirit; a broken and contrite heart, O God, thou wilt not despise" (Ps. 51:17). Four times Taylor quotes this verse as the first step in individual repentance, since the ancient Jewish poem as a whole celebrates before God the individual's responsibility for his own acts of mind and body.

If none of us is born evil, then this predilection we have for evil cannot be a consequent of Adam's sin. To be good all the time goes against our 'nature': we are not built for temperance, abstinence, patience, humility, self-denial, but have to strive for these virtues—or else merely yield to our 'condition.'

Despite Adam, then, we can still choose to sin or not to sin, and among several goods or evils choose one or several. The contrary would destroy all law, rewards and punishments.

This is plainly Biblical, too. After the fall, man "knew what nakedness was, and had experience of the difference of things, he perceived the evil and mischief of disobedience and the divine anger; he knew fear and flight, new apprehensions, and the trouble of a guilty conscience" (p. 279). Therefore, "to deny to the will of man powers of choice and election . . . destroys the [blissful] immortality of the soul" (p. 280), and this is what the extreme Calvinistic doctrine of original sin does.

Thus Taylor's ethical argument embraces an accurate view of man's existentialist state. That we are born to suffer and to die is a condition of life, not a punishment for a sin we did not commit. He adds Pliny to Seneca as pagan witness to what we know from the Bible: "The creature . . . begins his life with punishments, for no fault, but that he was born" (p. 285). From an ethical point of view, lack of righteousness in ourselves is not a thing but a lack of a thing and hence is no sin. Concupiscence, similarly, is neither sin nor evil before we consent to it. Our spirit can do nothing without the miracle of grace, partly because of our natural impotency and partly because of our folly. For the first we have Jesus Christ, and of the second we cannot complain (p. 288).

For their undermining the necessity to make ethical choices, certain Roman Catholic doctrines and practices come under Taylor's hammer. One is the distinction between venial and mortal sins: a sin is a sin, Taylor says, and two sins may differ in degree of magnitude but never in kind. Another practice is the deathbed repentance, justified by some with Christ's forgiving the thief on the cross at Golgotha. But this was the thief's first opportunity to repent, and he chose it. We who are given all our lives deceive ourselves by postponing repentance until the last minute. Finally, Taylor scores Jesuitical probabilism, and substitutes for it probabiliorism, which, demanding a choice between the less and the more probable consequences of every act, leads us to find arguments more in favor of liberty than of the law.

As in faith there are first cognizance and then the will to accept and act, so in sin there are the sense of it and the willingness to act or not. "The fathers before St. Augustine" (Taylor keeps to the pre-Augustinian tradition) insist on the doctrine of man's liberty after the fall to choose: Justin Martyr, Cyril, Jerome, Gregory of Nyssa, Ambrose (pp. 313–14). And this is "agreeable to nature, to experience, to the sentence of all wise men, to the nature of laws, to the effect of reward and punishments" (p. 314). There is no natural necessity for us to sin, only a free choice to sin or not to sin.

The ethical argument is a strong one, since Taylor, reminded always of God's economy, is always practical. "That's a good repentance that bears fruit, and not that which produces leaves only," he wrote in another context:

> When the heathen gods were to choose what trees they would have sacred to them and used in their festivals, Jupiter chose the oak, Venus the myrtle, Apollo loved the laurel, but wise Minerva took the Olive . . . the Olive gives an excellent fruit, fit for food and physick, which when Jupiter observed, he kissed his daughter, and called her wise: for all pompousness is vain, and the solemn religion stands for nothing, unless that which we do, be profitable and good for material uses (IX, xx).

To believe that because of Adam we cannot help doing evil is to surrender ethical choice and with it the opportunity to repent of the sins which we, not Adam, commit, and thus to miss the opportunity to be forgiven for them.

To summarize Adam's ethical condition: he was left in a state of nature, still free after the fall to choose good or evil. By that first sin we are not wholly defiled. In all of us there are still inclinations for good and for evil (cf. *Deus*, sec. iv). This state of nature only we inherit by nature from Adam after God deprived him of superadded grace, but God has since given us Jesus Christ, who promises forgiveness to all who freely choose to repent of their sins and are willing thereby to be saved.

III

This brings Taylor to his final and most important argument, not against original sin—he never denies the existence of original sin—but against the Calvinistic assumption of total depravity: it denigrates God's wisdom, justice, and love. A father himself and made even more sensitive to the ordinary human attachments within the family by successive deaths of his own children, Taylor is eloquent on the subject of the damnation of infants. "To condemn infants to hell for the fault of another," he cries, "is to deal worse with them than God did to the very devils, who did not perish but for an act of their own most perfect choice" (p. 255). And he caps his assertion that God does not damn anyone merely for the sin of our first father with a quotation from St. Ambrose's commentary on Romans, chapter 5: "*Mors autem dissolutio corporis est . . . sed eius occasione propriis peccatis acquiretur*—death is the dividing soul and body; there is also another death which is in hell, and is called the second death, which we do not suffer for the sin of Adam, but by occasion of it we fall into it by our own sins" (p. 257).

Anticipating what later was called "guilt by association," Taylor argues for the honor of God in that He never imputes a sin to a whole race on account of the commission of sin by a single individual or group. God in the Old Testament may visit evil on a son as judge not of the son but of the father, but since Christ came, God surrendered this right of dominion, for Christ came to plead for us; and here Taylor quotes the Latin of the Jewish Simeon Barsema which he found in Hugo Grotius's *De Jure Belli et Pacis* (p. 274).

Like Milton, then, Taylor must "justify the ways of God to man." Calvinistic doctrines of original sin, whether among most of the Presbyterians and Independents of his day or some of his fellow Anglicans, impute to God motives which it were a sin to impute to our fellow man. The worst doctrine is supralapsarianism, that God is pleased to damn persons even before they are born—like the Roman lictors who, not being allowed

86

to execute virgins, ravished Sejanus's daughters so that they could legally murder them (p. 501). Supralapsarians make God out to be not good, not just, and not reasonable. The more wary and temperate Calvinists, such as the followers of Gomarus at the Council of Dort, assert that God reprobates most people but chooses a few others for salvation. Still other Calvinists, those at the Westminster Assembly, assert that corruption of nature remains even in the regenerate, and though it may be pardoned through Christ, still it is a sin which Adam's guilt has brought upon us all. The passion with which Taylor fought all these forms of Calvinism is shown in a sentence from *Deus Justificatus:* "I have, I confess, heartily opposed it, and shall, besides my arguments, *confute it with my blood, if God shall call me;* for it is so great a reproach to the Spirit and power of Christ, and to the effects of baptism, to scripture and to right reason, that all good people are bound in conscience to be zealous against it" (p. 508, my italics).

To him supralapsarianism and sublapsarianism are one and the same in that both make God out to be willful and unjust: he who does a thing for a reason which he himself invents may as well do it without reason; and Taylor quotes both Calvin and Dr. Twisse on this point (p. 503). There follows a plea to a mother not to murder her child because it was born in London or on a Friday:

> Now madam consider, could you have in your heart when the nurse and midwives had bound up the heads of any of your children, when you have borne them with pain and joy upon your knees, could you have been tempted to give command that murderers should be brought to flay them alive, to put them to exquisite tortures, and then in the midst of their saddest groans, throw any one of them into the flames of a fierce fire, for no other reason but because he was born at London, or upon a Friday, when the moon was in her prime, or for what other reason you have made, and they could never avoid? Could you have been delighted in their horrid shrieks and outcries, or have taken pleasure in their unavoidable and their intolerable calam-

ity? Could you have smiled if the hangman had snatched your eldest son from his nurse's breasts, and dashed his brains out against the pavement; and would you not have wondered that any father or mother could espy the innocence and pretty smiles of your sweet babes, and yet tear their limbs in pieces, or devise devilish artifices to make them roar with intolerable convulsions? Could you desire to be thought good, and yet have delighted in such cruelty? I know I may answer for you; you would first have died yourself (p. 504).

Yet some Anglicans, even in high position, say that honor is given to God by virtue of Christ's wiping away the sin we inherit from Adam. Even this violates our sense of justice, for if man is not liable to damnation, how can he be liable to pardon? If it is against God's goodness that any should die eternally for original sin, then it is also against His justice that He can pardon us for it. He in whom Christ rules is forgiven the sins which he commits; otherwise Taylor's fellow Anglicans would have God more angry with Cain for being born than for murdering his brother. And there follows an analogy with the birds of paradise in the Molucca Islands:

Mankind now taken in his whole constitution and design, is like the birds of paradise which travellers tell us of in the Molucca islands; born without legs, but by a celestial power they have a recompense made to them for that defect; and they always hover in the air and feed on the dew of heaven: so are we birds of paradise, but cast out from thence, and born without legs, without strength to walk in the laws of God or to go to heaven; but by a power from above we are adopted in our new birth to a celestial conversation, we feed on the dew of heaven (p. 517).

Now (to pick up the argument which we left at the end of section 1) Taylor must argue on religious grounds against those Anglicans who, though they agree with him that we inherit original righteousness, yet insist on Article IX as part of the "Anglican creed." It is not. Article IX was adopted in 1562 to make peace with the Calvinists against the Roman Catholics at a particular juncture in history; and the Thirty-nine Articles should be read and are read (since they form no part of worship) with the same spirit of latitude with which they were originally agreed upon. That Taylor dared to renounce Article IX on "Original Sin" seemed more heinous to Bishop Warner than anything else he said. It follows:

> ix. Of Original or Birth-Sin.
> Original sin standeth not in the following of Adam, (as the Pelagians do vainly talk;) but it is the fault and corruption of the Nature of every man, that naturally is engendered of the offspring of Adam; whereby man is very far gone from original righteousness, and is of his own nature inclined to evil, so that the flesh lusteth always contrary to the Spirit; and therefore in every person born into this world, it deserveth God's wrath and damnation. And this infection of nature doth remain, yea in them that are regenerated; whereby the lust of the flesh, called in Greek φρονημα σαρκος (which some do expound the wisdom, some sensuality, some the affection, some the desire, of the flesh), is not subject to the Law of God. And although there is no condemnation for them that believe and are baptized; yet the Apostle doth confess, that concupiscence and lust hath of itself the nature of sin.

If it is intolerable to damn children for the sin of Adam (and Taylor's emphasis upon children throughout the controversy is not sentimental but theological—if God is in fact the Father), then it is intolerable that the sin itself be damnable, since sentence and execution are the same issue in God's justice. If by Adam we fall into a damnable condition, then when are we freed of that guilt? At the time of our baptism? If so, anyone who dies before baptism must suffer eternal torment, and what kind of God visits this upon a child? Taylor believes that we are born free, so that we are never charged with that guilt: Christ came to save mankind, and Christ satisfies all sins, including Adam's. Only, and this is part of the essential synergistic principle, motivated by His grace we must of ourselves come to Christ even as Mary *chose* to sit at His feet to hear His word.

It is more probable (*probabilior*) that children should be born beloved and quitted of wrath than that they should be born hated and condemned in Adam. We would be foolish to honor a physician for curing us of a disease we never had, or praise the Father's mercy for wounding us in order that His Son may have the honor to bind up the wound. It is simply bad economy to make a necessity for the purpose of finding a remedy. It dishonors God to think He works this way. Taylor's Christian creed in all this is simple and would run like this: I believe that we are left natural by Adam, that Christ is revealed as having come to do for us what our nature cannot do by itself: give us a new birth, a victory over death, grace, life, spirit, pardon for our own iniquities when we repent of them, and promise of everlasting glory. Amen.

As for the Articles on original sin in *The Book of Common Prayer*, in view of the anticipation by Taylor of several aspects of twentieth-century thinking, it is interesting that in the spirit of ecumenicity there is, at present, an Anglican move to expunge all Thirty-nine Articles from *The Book of Common Prayer*, including, of course, phrases that in 1562 united the Presbyterians and Anglicans as Protestants against Rome: "we are justified by Faith only" (XI); "the Church of Rome hath erred" (XIX); "the Romish Doctrine [of Purgatory]" (XXII); "Transubstantiation . . . is repugnant . . . and hath given occasion to many superstititions" (XXVIII); "the sacrifices of Masses . . . [are] blasphemous fables, and dangerous deceits" (XXXI). All these phrases and more in *The Book of Common Prayer* in 1970 now serve only to separate Christian communions, Taylor would say, and thus are a dishonor to God.

This ends Taylor's argument aginst the Calvinistic concept of original sin. On the grounds of right reason (which his whole education inured him to) and "the liberty of prophesying" (which entailed a verse-by-verse rational exegesis of Romans, chapter 5), and of the tradition of the Christian church before St. Augustine "invented" predestined damnation in order to derogate man as an answer to Pelagian humanism, Taylor built his argument. That his view of the problem is true answers the superficial objection that it is new, for that a thing is new is nothing against it so long as it is true. And, as a matter of fact, Taylor's views are not new. Even if Taylor's views were true, what is the necessity, cries Bishop Duppa, of disturbing the ecclesiastical peace? Truth is preferable to peace any day, especially the truth of God to the peace of man. Next, Taylor's view of original sin allows man to lead a better life. It can prepare him for repentance and so forgiveness; it does away with the excesses of spiritual pride and antinomianism which predestinarianism often brings in its train. Finally, after it is true, after it is ethically useful, it is more religious in restoring the honor to God which the doctrine of reprobation takes away from Him. "My proposition," Taylor avers, ". . . I am most sure is . . . zealous for God's honour, and the reputation of His justice, and wisdom, and goodness" (p. 19). The polemic on original sin against the Reprobationists was one of Taylor's own choosing, against formidable opponents, and conducted at the most inopportune moment in England's church history and at a time when Taylor himself could lose his own liberty and even his life for it.

Taylor's argument not only had to be countered by two Anglican bishops, but it brought the wrath of the whole Presbyterian faction down on his head. Among others, the Reverend John Gaule, Presbyterian clergyman of Staughton, Huntingdonshire, mocked one of Taylor's titles in *Sapientia Justificata* in 1657. The following year, the Presbyterian minister at Fanny Drayton, Leicestershire, attacked Taylor's ideas on original sin in *Vindiciae Fundamenti*. The Anglican Herbert Thorndike, believing that Taylor had sounded the death knell of his own church, published the year before the Restoration of Charles II, *An Epilogue to the Church of England*. In 1665, Taylor's views of original sin were still worth refuting for Edward Worseley, who published *Truth Will Out*. The counterarguments are already so familiar from the history of the concept of original sin that we need speak here in a little more detail about only two of the contemporary Presbyterian rejoinders.

Anthony Burgesse had already begun *A Treatise of Original Sin* (London, 1658) when Taylor published his first daring challenges. In his preface "To the Christian Reader," Burgesse includes Jeremy Taylor among "Those who attend to Aristotle more than Paul, and desire to be rationales, rather than fideles; [they] have grossely stumbled in the darke they walke in." "More particularly," he continues, "a late English Writer Dr. Taylor . . . like a second Julian in triumphing language, hath with much boldness and audacity decried [the concept of original sin]."[40] Hence Taylor complies "with Pelagius and some Jesuits in that notion":

> What learning and abilities the Author may have, I do not detract from, only it's greatly to be lamented, that he should contrary to Cyprian and others, take the Gold he had in Jerusalem, and carry it into Egypt to build an Idol there. He hath fully improved his liberty of Prophesying, and waving reverence to the Scriptures, Councils, and Fathers, yea, and the Church of England . . . by a sceptical and academic disposition, he is fallen into this Heresie. . . . Neither let the Writer think that his industrous affectation of words and language, will make falshood to be truth. There is a great difference between skin and bone, words and arguments in any Theological Discourse.[41]

Leveling the charge of heresy against Taylor in 1658, Burgesse pays a backhanded compliment to one of his famous works and to his skill in language. Burgesse attempts to argue against him, mostly by quoting texts and sometimes by a rhetorical display of his own. But his major weapon against Taylor is name-calling:

> When I had proceeded farre in this Discourse of Original Sinne there cometh but an English Writer (Dr. J. Taylor Unum Necess.) in a triumphing and scoreful style, like Julian of old, peremptorily opposing this Doctrine of in-

herent pollution by Nature. He is not merely Pelagian, Arminian, Papist, or Socinian, but an hotchpotch of all . . . this man most unhappily sometimes select[s] what is most deformed in those several parties.[42]

As far as we know Taylor paid no attention to all this. He did pay attention to another opponent, the Reverend Henry Jeanes of Chedzoy, Somersetshire, who directly challenged Taylor in letters and then, without permission, published the correspondence. Jeanes had been an Anglican but with the shift in power turned Presbyterian. His predecessor at Chedzoy, the Reverend Walter Raleigh, had left his vicarage to attend the king. In 1645, when General Fairfax's forces approached, Dean Raleigh was at Bridgewater; when it fell to the Parliamentary army, he was set on a horse with his legs tied under its belly and led back to his own vicarage, for it was to become Fairfax's headquarters. To fill the vacancy in the adjoining church, Henry Jeanes, who had once been Anglican vicar at Kingston, was chosen as a strong upholder now of Presbyterianism.[43]

Jeanes had been a brilliant student at Cambridge and was a well-known controversialist, but he should never have tangled with Taylor. The correspondence clearly shows the greater scholar's initial patience and charity crumbling before sheer intransigeance. After reading *Unum Necessarium*, Jeanes expressed himself to "one Mr. T.C." (whom I cannot identify) as shocked by the "nonsense and blasphemy" of its views on original sin. "Mr. T.C. brake out into extraordinary (that I say not excessive and hyperbolical) praises of Dr. Jeremy Taylor," Jeanes tells us. Rather than discuss the issues between them, the guest agreed to become a middleman between the two theologians, and thus the correspondence began. In 1660 Jeanes published it as *Certain Letters of Henry Jeanes, Minister of God's Word at Chedzoy, and Dr. Jeremy Taylor, concerning a Passage of his in Further Explication of Original Sin*. Be it to Mr. Jeanes's credit that, unlike Anthony Burgesse, he did grasp the tripartite shape of Taylor's whole argument: that the Presbyterian view of original sin is not true, does not lead to a holy life, and dishonors God. In his main attempt to refute, Jeanes calls Taylor's view nonsense: that is, it violates logic or truth. Next, he calls it dangerous to the ethical life: "this tenet is chargeable with libertinism." Finally, Jeanes "charge[s] it with blasphemy; it blasphemes three acts of God" (VII, 574).

But he is no match. When he tries some technical ploys in logic, Taylor demolishes them. Jeanes then takes Taylor's answers personally and defends himself rather than the issues. Taylor answers in kind to the charge of blasphemy, and "If you please, you may take time to consider it; but in the interim, if you be pleased to read a little discourse of mine, called *Deus Justificatus*, you shall find my question not to be answered by you, if you have any regard to the authority or to the reason of Mr. Calvin, Dr. Twisse, and some other bigots of your party" (VII, 583).

Tired of attempting to convince him, Taylor said he was too busy with other and more important things and wanted to hear no more from Dr. Jeanes of Chedzoy on original sin (p. 585). Almost two hundred years later, the Reverend R. A. Willmott deplored Taylor's decision: "In this manner was a controversy conducted, respecting one of the darkest mysteries of our nature; and thus was the presence of sin manifested in the inquiry of its origin."[44]

But Taylor was preparing for the press his final work, the longest and most compendious of his career, the *Ductor Dubitantium* on cases of conscience. The last stumbling block to Christian repentance, the Reprobationist interpretation of original sin, had been removed. In the heat of battle this usually gentle and modest scholar raised a banner emblazoned with a legend so extraordinary that it deserves capital letters:

"THIS GORDIAN KNOT I HAVE NOW UNTIED, AS ALEXANDER DID, BY DESTROYING IT AND CUTTING IT ALL IN PIECES" (p. 283).

Some Last Things

V

In the summer of 1658 Taylor arrived in North Ireland to take up a minor post as "lecturer" in the small parish of Lisnagarvey (Lisburn). Such a position entailed only the duty of preaching, usually in rotation with others, and not of being in full charge, like a rector of a parish. Taylor had been reluctant to accept the appointment. With obvious reference to the famous precedent of Richard Hooker's altercation with the Presbyterian Travers at the Temple, he wrote to John Evelyn on May 12, 1658: "I like not the condition of being a lecturer under the dispose of another, nor to serve in my semi-circle, where a presbyterian and myselfe shall be like Castor and Pollux, the one up and the other down" (I, lxxviii). But Lord Conway, within whose Irish estate the parish lay, had urged and persuaded; he had even procured Cromwell's protection for Taylor (who had served his prison term) and his family. Under these auspices and the pressure of his own impoverished circumstance, Taylor finally accepted.

From the outset the learned doctor found little support among the local population. And even after the Restoration, when Taylor had become a bishop, vice-chancellor of the University of Dublin, and a member of the Irish Privy Council, he had still to contend, in all these positions, with Presbyterian and Roman Catholic opposition. As a human being he returned their suspicion and hostility, at least in letters to England. He referred to the Presbyterians as "Scotch spiders," and wrote of the others: "The Roman religion is here amongst us a faction, and a state party, and a design to recover their old laws and barbarous manner of living . . . . And if this be religion, it is such an one as ought to be reproved by all the severities of reason and religion, lest the people perish . . ." (I, cxvii).

Upon the Restoration of the king he must have expected a bishopric in England, for among the Anglican clergy who were swiftly appointed on the advice of Sheldon lest the apostolic succession die out, Taylor was one of the most learned and eloquent. More importantly, in three controversies during the Civil War he had risked even his life for the cause. On December 19, 1660, he wrote from Dublin to the duke of Ormond about the ministers in his own diocese who "have gone about to asperse me as an Arminian, and a Socinian, and a papist." "I am not at all guilty," he continued, "as having no other religion but that of the church of England, . . . *for which I have often stood up an advocate against all opposition*" (I, ci, my italics).

In effect he was exiled to Ireland by being consecrated bishop of Down and Connor in St. Patrick's Cathedral on January 18, 1661. Gosse gives an unfortunate slant to Taylor's episcopal behavior, accusing him among other things of going back on his own principles stated in *The Liberty of Prophesying* in order to disallow any opinion different from his own among the clergy and people of Down, Connor, and Dromore.[1] This has been corrected by Frederick R. Bolton in *The Caroline Tradition of the Church of Ireland, with particular Reference to Jeremy Taylor*.[2] With careful documentation, Bolton shows that Taylor was not less conciliatory than others. Of seventy Presbyterian ministers occupying "Anglican" pulpits, about one-half were in his diocese at the time of the Restoration; Taylor's Lord Primate Bramhall had to make more replacements, consequently, in Down, Connor, and Dromore than in "all the other dioceses [in Ireland] put together."[3]

Taylor himself ordained more Presbyterian ministers than any other bishop in Ireland during the years of his tenure. Bolton also argues convincingly that Taylor was not aloof, embittered, and rebellious, but showed many expressions of understanding and kindness. Bolton refutes Hugh Ross Williamson's implication (by analogy with Dean Swift?) that in his final years Taylor suffered mental illness.

Taylor was a very busy bishop and hardly had time to engage in petty feuds, even had such behavior been part of his personality. He served on various church and state committees, working closely with Bramhall, whose funeral sermon he was to preach on July 16, 1663. He was writing and overseeing new editions of former works. He preached often and still well enough to have his sermons survive in print. He attended meetings of the Irish Privy Council, and immersed himself in University affairs. And yet he must share the blame with his Anglican co-workers for refusing to have services conducted in the native Irish language for those country folk who understood neither Latin nor English.

Especially in Ireland evidence of Taylor's reputation as a controversialist keeps appearing. As Marjorie Nicolson puts it, "the fighter in Taylor came to the fore, and for the last half dozen years, he fought valiantly in the service of 'his Majesty and the Church.' "[4] He seemed to invite replies by some of his titles, *A Dissuasive from Popery*, for example. One such was written by an anonymous Roman Catholic: *A Letter to a Friend, touching Dr. Jeremy Taylor's Dissuasive from Popery, Discovering above an Hundred and fifty False, or Wrested Quotations in it. Psal. 26:12. Mentita est iniquitas sibi. Printed in the Year, 1665*. The author praises Taylor among his Anglican confreres as "a man so eminent among them for Place, Learning, and Abilities in Controversie. . . ."[5] Who would expect such a man to make mistakes? The worst one occurs in "The Life of Christ" where Taylor refers (II, 339) by "chapter and verse" to St. Gregory's telling of "St. Hermengilda" choosing to die rather than to receive the blessed sacrament from an Arian bishop. "Any of our women could have told him [Taylor] the person in S. Gregory was not a woman but a man, Hermengildus, Prince of Spain."[6]

Taylor longed for England. Aware of the stand he had taken on original sin and supposing it (I think rightly) to have been responsible for blocking his legitimate ambitions, he wrote to Archbishop Sheldon from Portmore on May 25, 1664: "I have been informed from a good hand in England, that your grace was pleased to say, that I myself was the only hindrance to myself of being removed to an English bishopric" (I, cxix). Though he labored dutifully to meet his many public responsibilities, it is understandable that his interests and loyalties should have remained with earlier, more congenial associates, including Mrs. Katharine Phillips "the Matchless Orinda," George Rust from early Cambridge days, Henry More, and John Evelyn.

He died at the age of fifty-five on August 13, 1667, and lies buried in the little cathedral of Christ Church, which he helped build at Lisburn. He was only the fifth bishop of the fairly recent Anglican diocese, having been preceded by John Todd (1607), James Dunbar (1612), Robert Echlin (1613), and Henry Leslie (1635). His immediate successor was Roger Boyle (1667). In the same church is buried a later successor who became famous in literature, Thomas Percy (1724–1811), bishop of Down and Connor for thirty years. In 1765 he published his collection of ballads known as "Percy's Reliques of Ancient English Poetry."

On the episcopal chair in this church is inscribed: "Beneath this lie the remains of Jeremy Taylor, Bishop of Dromore 1661 to 1667," and "*In piam memoriam Jeremy Taylor S.T.P., eruditi Theologici, diserti oratoris, fidelis Pastoris, hujus Diocesis Episcopi. A.D. 1661-1667.*" The present dean's study contains a portrait of Taylor painted by Frank MacKelvey from an early engraving. In the east window of the church, inscribed "Te Deum Laudamus," among archangels, prophets, Holy Innocents, saints, and martyrs shine the figures of Martin Luther, Archbishop Cranmer, and Jeremy Taylor.

It was a custom in the seventeenth century for ambitious but minor poets to praise famous men upon their death. And so in Dublin appeared *A Pindarique Elegie upon the Death of the R.R. Father in God Jeremy, Late Lord Bishop of Doune, Connor, and Dromore. By Le. Mathews A.M. a sacr. domest. Dublin, Printed by John Crook . . . and are to be sold by Samuel Dancer, Bookseller in Castlestreet, 1667:*

> Such was the man whom all admir'd,
> Whom Fame and Heaven's sweet breath inspir'd,
> Whose funeral voice made others live,
> And immortality did often give (*stanza ii, p. 6*).

> He was the man so pure, so innocent,
> So careless of forbidden fruit,
> Richly supply'd with Nature's own recruit;
> So masculine his soul, so content
> To be but man; so little bent
> To vice, that you might call
> Him one not bruis'd by *Adam's* fall (*stanza iv, p. 7*).

> So vast his knowledge, he
> Had tasted oft of each allowed tree,
> For's tongue had all the charms of words,
> All that language and wit affords,
> And new and fitter names did wear,
> And's lucky pen (as if a pencil 'twere)
> Made gold, by guil'ng it, more golden to appear
>   (*stanza v, p. 8*).

In the year of his death, Taylor is thus hailed as famous, pious, learned, eloquent, and so good as to be practically unstained by original sin. At the end, the "poet" imagines his subject entering heaven:

> He gently passes, through
> A long admiring row
> Of sainted ghosts to martyr Charles's Wain.
> Come, *Taylor*, come:
> Here's *Hammond*, there is *Sanderson;*

The lesser Angels all make room,
And they embrace . . . (*stanza xii, p. 13*).

The method of analysis has made it difficult so far to separate Taylor's mind from his temper in argument, but the manner in which he conducted these arguments invites comparison with that of his great contemporary, Milton. After showing how antithetical the two were in subject matter and tone, Coleridge brings them together in this way: "Differing, then, so widely and almost contrarily, wherein did these great men agree? . . . In Genius, in Learning, in unfeigned Piety, in blameless Purity of Life, and in benevolent aspirations and purposes for the moral and temporal improvement of their fellow-creatures."[7] Coleridge's propensity for German metaphysics perhaps had made him impatient with Taylor's "latitude of Theologie," much of which depends on no "precise and cleere determination." Hence he did not recognize that Taylor does not deny original sin in Adam nor its effects upon us but only thinks that its pessimistic promulgation tends to deprive us of choice. Taylor and Milton are most importantly one on the freedom of the will.

But in the heat of controversy the "Arminian" Taylor is more even tempered than Milton, and never took pleasure in crushing a Salmasius. He had apparently heeded better than Milton a warning from Acontius, whose *Strategemata Satanae* (1565) teaches learned men how to conduct a Christian inquiry into truth. "Never be convinced that you know everything," Acontius says; for,

> Unhinged by this conviction you will not be able to suffer any man to utter a complete sentence: scarcely has he opened his mouth, when you will think you have fathomed what the other is going to say, and even what he might say. And with a single word—a word, do I say? nay rather, with a single laugh or grim look or gesture of some sort you think you have more than sufficiently explained away any objection that may have been raised; and if any one dare so much as to hint disagreement with anything you

have affirmed or denied, you regard him as guilty of high treason and sacrilege.[8]

In this respect Taylor was so gentle and so liberal in widening his views to accommodate the ordinary man's understanding that Coleridge almost makes him an arrant Pelagian. And yet, though both Milton and Taylor were extraordinarily learned, even in disputation Taylor is always the Christian divine and, like a good preacher, teacher, or marriage counselor, always practical. In his University of Dublin sermon, *Via Intelligentiae,* he contrasts man's way of attaining truth with God's way, thoroughly aware of his student audience:

> I know I am in an auditory of inquisitive persons, whose business is to study for truth, that they may find it for themselves and teach it unto others: I am in a school of prophets and prophets' sons, who all ask Pilate's question, "What is truth?" You look for it in your books, and you tug hard for it in your disputations, and you derive it from the cisterns of the fathers, and you enquire after the old ways, and sometimes are taken with new appearances, and you rejoice in false lights, or are delighted with little umbrages and peep of day (VIII, 367).

Each of us thinks that his is the one true way. Faced with the dilemma, Taylor suggests, man can choose among three main alternatives: (1) he can submit to an "infallible" guide, but there is none; or (2) he can be moderate and attempt to reconcile differences by wise and clear speaking, but others are stubborn; or (3) he can tolerate all opinions and buy peace at the price of believing nothing. None of these will work, for each is instigated by a sin, which is man's usual way. There remains God's way, and how do we find that? Mainly by living a life of religion: "Theology is rather a divine life than a divine knowledge. In heaven indeed we shall first see, and then love; but here on earth we must first love, . . . and we shall then see and perceive and understand" (VII, 368).

There remains the question of how relevant today are the ideas Taylor fought for during the Civil War in England over three hundred years ago. First, he would have agreed with Hooker that episcopacy as a church polity is not essential, but in Taylor's time it almost came to an end. Today episcopacy obtains in a worldwide Anglican communion. He loved liturgy, but himself changed *The Book of Common Prayer* to meet the exigency of its temporary proscription. Liturgy is still an important part of worship for many people, and great liturgists like Taylor are still slowly changing it to meet the changing needs of time. So much for his first controversy.

Second, for the toleration of differing religious opinions in a pluralistic society he is very modern indeed and plays a part in the history of the principle of "separation of church and state" in America. His *Liberty of Prophesying* still stands as one of the great documents of intellectual freedom, along with Milton's *Areopagitica* (1644), in which liberty is also limited in order to differentiate it from license.

As for his last controversy, Taylor has been attacked for his views on original sin, despite the fact that they were suggested by a host of predecessors going back to Tatian and Duns Scotus. For his interpretation of St. Paul's letter to the Romans, on which both sides of the argument stood, he was still being castigated in the nineteenth century by Coleridge, and even more harshly by Bishop Heber, his great editor and biographer.

Three present-day theologians, however—an Anglican, a Lutheran, and a Presbyterian—agree with Jeremy Taylor's interpretation of the doctrine of original sin as it is based on *The Epistle to the Romans*. One is the scholarly exegesis by the Right Reverend Dr. K. E. Kirk, bishop of Oxford, which has gone into four editions from 1937 to 1953.[9]

Again, Bishop Anders Nygren of Lund has written *A Commentary on Romans*, translated into English by C. C. Rasmussen. This contemporary Swedish scholar points out, apropos of Romans, chapter 5, that "Augustine and the theological tradition that builds on him cannot correctly understand what Paul means when he speaks of love."[10] Nygren asserts, with

Jeremy Taylor, that the theme of Romans (from Rom. 1:16–17) is "He who through faith is righteous shall live," and he analyzes Paul's epistle as a definition not of bondage but of FREEDOM: from the wrath of God (Rom. 5:1–21), from sin (Rom. 6:1–23), from the law (Rom. 7:1–25), from death (Rom. 8:1–39), for all believers (Rom. 9:1–11:36) who conduct themselves appropriately in the New Eon of Christ rather than in the Old Eon of Adam (Rom. 12:1–15:13).

Finally, in 1961 Bruce H. Throckmorton, Jr., in *Romans for the Layman* says: "The point we wish especially to emphasize is that nowhere in this Genesis story is it suggested that Adam and Eve passed on to their descendants an inherent moral weakness because of a change in their nature that took place when they sinned."[11] On Romans, chapter 5, Throckmorton says, "Man is not a sinner exclusively of necessity. If he were, he would not then be guilty, for one is not guilty because of having yielded to the necessary or inevitable."[12]

One might well wonder what all the fuss was about concerning original sin in the face of such agreement between Taylor and these three twentieth-century Biblical scholars. It was in 1655 that Jeremy Taylor boasted that he had "cut this Gordian knot." Apparently he had cut it well.

Taylor will remain alive in his poetic "gems" of English prose. But even these will be more rightly read if we have learned something from the present study of the man and the skill in language he attained under pressure. John Dryden once said, "They cannot be good poets who are not accustomed to argue well."[13] Taylor's bright similitudes issued from a mind sharpened by the arts of disputation and a heart that dared, in England's period of greatest religious and political turmoil, to argue his points against all opposition "with his blood if that were demanded."

Notes

CHAPTER I

1. Matthew Arnold, *Lectures and Essays in Criticism*, ed. R. H. Super (Ann Arbor, Mich., 1962), pp. 245–46.
2. (London, 1892), p. 233.
3. *The Whole Works of the Right Rev. Jeremy Taylor, D.D.*, edited by Reginald Heber [bishop of Calcutta] and revised by Charles P. Eden, 10 vols. (London, 1847–54). All quotations from Taylor will be from this edition, hereafter called Heber-Eden, with references in my text.
4. *A Relation of the Conference between William Laud . . . and Mr. Fisher, the Iesuit . . .* (London, 1639). Of this book Laud had written in his diary: "I had not hitherto appeared in print. I am no controvertist" [*Works*, III (Oxford, 1853), 147].
5. John Cosin, *Correspondence* (Durham, 1869), pt. I, p. 21.
6. Samuel R. Gardiner, *The History of the Great Civil War, 1642–1649* (London, 1891), V, 352.
7. Taylor consistently follows sermons, prayers, offices, etc., with "Practical Considerations." In this connection cf. H. R. McAdoo, *The Structure of Caroline Moral Theology* (London, 1949), pref., p. xi: "What strikes the moral theologian with fresh force the further he penetrates, is the universal interest of the seventeenth century in 'practical divinity' and the importance accorded to it officially and parochially throughout the period."
8. R. Cattermole, ed., *The Liberty of Prophesying by Jeremy Taylor* (London, 1834), introd., p. xii.

CHAPTER II

1. Cf. the seventeenth-century Anglican, the Reverend Herbert Thorndike, "Of the Principles of Christian Truth" in *Works, The Library of Anglo-Catholic Theology*, vol. 73, pt. 2 (Oxford, 1845), pp. 6–7: "The cause of Episcopacy and of the Service is the cause of the whole Church, and the Maintenance thereof inferreth the maintenance of whatsoever is Catholic." Exactly paralleling Taylor's double argument for the Anglican church, Thorndike published in 1641 *Of the Government of Churches, A Discourse pointing at the Primitive Forms;* and in 1642 *Of Religious Assemblies and the Public Service of God.*

2. In his dedication to Laud of the 1638 Gunpowder Sermon, Taylor writes: "It pleased some who had power to command me, to wish me to the publication of these my short and sudden meditations, that if it were possible even this way I might express my duty to God and the king" (Heber-Eden, I, xxii).

3. Benjamin Jowett, trans., *The Dialogues of Plato* (New York, 1939), II, 17.

4. "Literature," chap. xiv of *English Traits* (Boston, 1866), p. 238.

5. Cf. Walter Hilton, *The Ladder of Perfection*, trans. Leo Sherley-Price (Harmondsworth, 1957); and Joseph E. Milosh, *The Scale of Perfection and the English Mystical Tradition* (Madison, Wis., 1966), pp. 32–33.

6. The documents for this chapter are all in vol. V of Heber-Eden; hereafter only the page numbers to this volume will be incorporated in the text.

7. *Bibliotheca Biblica. Being a Commentary upon all the books of the Old and New Testament. Gather'd out of the genuine writings of Fathers and ecclesiastical historians, and acts of Councils. To which are added introductory discourses . . . with notes and scholia, etc.* [By Samuel Parker of T. C. Oxford, first five volumes only published at Oxford, 1720–35, from the 1611 version.]

8. According to the *Dictionnaire d'histoire et de géographie ecclésiastique* (Paris, 1912), the Acephali were called that by the Council of Chalcedonia in 451 A.D.; and Aerius was a bishop in Armenia in 355 A.D.

9. Here I depend on G. W. O. Addleshaw, *The High Church Tradition* (London, 1941).
10. Ed. 1637, p. 13.
11. *Ibid.*, p. 73.
12. George Herbert avoided reference to the altar controversy in *A Priest to the Temple*. Had he lived through 1637, however, even his irenic temper might have been challenged.
13. The phrase is a medieval colloquialism meaning "to get to the bottom of it." Cf. Chaucer, "NPT," line 420: "But I ne kan nat bulte it to the bren."

CHAPTER III

1. I use the text of Heber-Eden, vol. V; hereafter all quotations from *The Liberty of Prophesying* are from this volume, and only the page numbers will be incorporated in my text.
2. Edward Hyde, first earl of Clarendon, *The History of the Rebellion and Civil Wars in England* [XI, 40] (Oxford, 1958), IV, 345.
3. Virgil Heltzel, *Huntington Library Bulletin*, no. 11 (1937), pp. 61–62.
4. *The Structure of Caroline Moral Theology* (London, 1949), p. 6. It should be noted that in the first edition Taylor had maintained a better proportion of space between the two: about seventeen pages for the Anabaptists and about fourteen for the Roman Catholics. But when certain *Adversaria* were published on paedobaptism, he undertook to answer them so that in the second edition (1657) his section on the Anabaptists unfortunately attains to fifty-one pages.
5. Cf., for example, this sentence from *Holy Dying:* "A repentance upon our death-bed is like washing a corpse; it is cleanly and civil but makes no change deeper than the skin" (III, 372). Cf. IV, 381–407.
6. It is surprising to note that Rutherford should become in our day one of the apostles of liberty in Marcus L. Loane, *Makers of Religious Freedom in the Seventeenth Century: Henderson, Rutherford, Bunyan, Baxter* (Grand Rapids, Mich., 1961).

7. Samuel R. Gardiner, *History of the Great Civil War, 1642–1649* (London, 1891), III, 136.
8. Des Maiseaux's *Life of Chillingworth* (1725), p. 50; cf. Heber's note, I, ccliii.
9. Sir Edmund Gosse, *Jeremy Taylor* (London, 1904), p. 43.
10. *Letters*, p. 233, as quoted by W. K. Jordan, *The Development of Religious Toleration in England* (Cambridge, Mass., 1938), III, 505.

CHAPTER IV

1. H. P. Wyndham, *A Gentleman's Tour through Monmouthshire and Wales* (London, 1781), p. 3.
2. Thomas Carlyle, *Cromwell's Letters and Speeches* (London, 1904), III, 453.
3. *The Diary and Correspondence of John Evelyn*, ed. William Bray and revised by Henry Wheatley (Oxford, 1906), II, 50.
4. *Ibid.*, p. 51.
5. *Ibid.*, III, 204.
6. *Ibid.*, II, 76.
7. *Ibid.* In this connection Evelyn gave this advice in his *Memoirs for my Grand-Son:* "And here I counsel you to make a choice of some pious and learned Divine to whom you may also have recourse for Advice and Direction in matters relating to Conscience" [ed. Sir Geoffrey Keynes (London, 1926), p. 34].
8. B. D. Greenslade, "Jeremy Taylor in 1655," *N & Q* CXCVI (March 17, 1951), 130.
9. Thomas Richards, *Religious Developments in Wales, 1654–1662* (London, 1923), p. 282.
10. *Diary*, ed. Bray-Wheatley, II, 81.
11. *Ibid.*, II, 90.
12. *Ibid.*, III, 206. On the dating of this letter Wheatley follows Heber, who in "Note O" (I, cclxxvi-vii) realized that the date could not be March 18, 1655, since it was on that day that Evelyn heard Taylor preach in London; hence Heber conjectures that "18 Mar." may be a mistake for "18 Mai." I think it unlikely that a diarist would mistake March for May; that the greater likelihood is a confusion between old and new calendar

Notes to Pages 66–72

styles, the correct date being "18 Mar. 1655/6," which for us is 1656. Particulars in the letter demand more time than that between March and May of the same year. Most importantly, since the Cromwellian edict Evelyn is writing about took effect on Christmas Day, 1655, this letter could not have been written either in March or in May of 1655.

13. *Diary*, ed. Bray-Wheatley, III, 207. I cannot understand Wheatley's dating of this letter "Novem: 21, 1665." Even were there a careless transposition of the last two figures, which is likely, making the year "1656" instead of "1665," November seems rather late for an answer to the kind of letter sent in March. In Wheatley, this letter to Evelyn from Taylor is placed directly after the one it obviously answers, which I date "18 Mar., 1656."

14. *Diary*, III, 208–9.
15. *Ibid.*, II, 83.
16. *Ibid.*, III, 211.
17. My main secondary sources for this section have been the articles on original sin in *The New Catholic Encyclopedia* (1967); James Hastings's *Encyclopedia of Religion and Ethics;* F. R. Tennant, *The Concept of Sin* (Cambridge, 1912); and Norman P. Williams, *The Ideas of the Fall and Original Sin* (London, 1929).
18. *British Reformers*, CVIII (Philadelphia, 1842), 269.
19. P. H. Ditchfield, *The Church in the Netherlands* (London, 1893).
20. *Golden Remains* (London, 1673). Introductory Letter.
21. For an account of Castellio's part in the history of liberal theology in its fight against mental and physical persecution, cf. Roland H. Bainton, "Sebastian Castellio and the Toleration Controversy of the Sixteenth Century," *Persecution and Liberty: Essays in Honor of George Lincoln Burr* (New York, 1931), pp. 183–209.
22. Cf. Etienne Giran, *Sébastien Castellion et la réforme calviniste* (Haarlem and Paris, 1914), pp. 434–80.
23. *The Writings of Arminius*, ed. W. R. Bagnall (Grand Rapids, Mich., 1956); vols. I and II trans. by James Nichols (London, 1925–28), and vol. III trans. by Bagnall.

24. *Ibid.*, III, 13.
25. *Ibid.*, III, 100.
26. *Ibid.*, III, 281–525.
27. That Taylor was steeped in Arminianism is shown by almost everything he wrote, and by his list of books for a theological library drawn up in 1660: in this list he singles out "Episcopius, whose whole works are excellent, and containe the whole body of orthodox religion" (Heber-Eden, I, lxxxix).
28. 1634 ed., p. A 2 v.
29. Just how much Taylor admired the Remonstrant position on original sin at the Council of Dort is shown in the same bibliographical letter of 1660 wherein he writes: "I very much commend to you a little booke called *Declaratio sententiae eorum qui ex foederato Belgio vocantur Remonstrantes*, together with the *Apologia* they published in defence of it."
30. I use a rare edition of *The Directory* owned by Princeton University, a small 8vo dated 1651 with no cover or title page. On p. A 2 r appears "The Acts of the General Assembly approving the Confession of Faith, Edinburgh 27. August, 1647." My quotation of the six key points is found on pp. 16–17.
31. *Ibid.*, pp. 25–26.
32. *Ibid.*, pp. 79–80.
33. *Collection of Tracts Concerning Predestination* (London, 1719), p. 244.
34. A minor ironic note on William Twisse is this: along with the skeletons of twenty others (including Admiral Robert Blake and John Pym) who had been buried within the chapels and college of St. Peter in Westminster, his bones were ordered on September 10, 1661, by Charles II to be exhumed and thrown into St. Margaret's churchyard. Not until December 16, 1966, were they 'sanctified' by a suitable service and commemorated by a tablet erected by The Cromwell Association. The main speaker on this occasion was Sir Dingle Foot, Q.C., M.P., solicitor general in H.M. government and son of the founder of The Cromwell Association.
35. (Oxford, 1653), p. 4 v.
36. Ed., *The Golden Grove* (Oxford, 1930), p. xxviii.
37. Hereafter in this section references by page number alone to Heber-Eden, vol. VII, will be incorporated. In Taylor's quota-

tion of sources I have not felt obliged to give references since Eden has established them well in his notes to Heber.

38. *The Decline of Hell: Seventeenth Century Discussions of Eternal Torment* (London, 1964).

39. It is interesting that there should be firm agreement between Taylor and C. J. Peter, the author of the article on original sin in *The New Catholic Encyclopedia* (1967); cf. his final sentence (X, 781): "A truly superhuman, or God-like, condition was present in humanity originally, at least by divine offer; it was lost, possibly in the first moment of truly human existence, only to be reoffered in restoration to all men by Christ."

40. (London, 1658), p. A 3 r.

41. *Ibid.*

42. *Ibid.*, p. 30.

43. *The Victoria History of Somerset* (London, 1906), II, 47–48; and *Walker's Sufferings of the Clergy*, rev. by A. G. Matthew (Oxford, 1948).

44. *Bishop Jeremy Taylor* (London, 1847), p. 151.

CHAPTER V

1. Edmund Gosse, *Jeremy Taylor* (London, 1903).

2. (London, 1958), pp. 34–35. A previous correction of Gosse had appeared in less detail in Matthew Beckett, *Sir George Rawdon* [Lord Conway's brother-in-law] (Belfast, 1935).

3. Bolton, p. 270.

4. Ed., *The Conway Letters* (New Haven, 1930), p. 121.

5. (1665), p. A 2.

6. *Ibid.*, "The Publisher to the Reader."

7. Quoted by Roberta Florence Brinkley, ed., *Coleridge on the Seventeenth Century* (Durham, N.C., 1955), p. 315. Despite Coleridge's disagreement with Taylor on original sin, he obviously loved the man as Lamb did. Thomas Love Peacock, however, in "The Four Ages of Poetry" lumps Jeremy Taylor together with various ingredients to form the 'drooling school': "Mr. Wordsworth picks up village legends from old women and sextons; and Mr. Coleridge, to the valuable information acquired from similar sources, superadds the dreams of crazy theologians and the mysticisms of German metaphysics, and

111

favours the world with visions in verse, in which the guadruple elements of sexton, old woman, Jeremy Taylor, and Emanuel Kant, are harmonized into a delicious poetical compound" [*Prose of the Romantic Period*, ed. Carl Woodring (New York, 1961), p. 578].

8. Acontius, *Satan's Strategems*, trans. Walter T. Curtis (San Francisco, 1940), p. 50.
9. *The Epistle to the Romans* (Oxford, 1937, 1947, 1950, 1953).
10. (Philadelphia, 1949), p. 199.
11. (Philadelphia, 1961), p. 46.
12. *Ibid.*, p. 55.
13. In the course of the controversy with his brother-in-law Sir Robert Howard over *An Essay of Dramatick Poesy* (1668); *Essays of John Dryden*, ed. W. P. Ker (Oxford, 1926), I, 121.

Bibliography

NOTE: *This bibliography is divided into three sections: (a) texts of the seventeenth century and earlier; (b) books and articles on Jeremy Taylor since his time; and (c) general works on the religious, political, and literary milieu.*

Texts of the Seventeenth Century and Earlier

Acontius. *Satan's Strategems . . . with an epistle by . . . J[ohn] G[oodwin] . . . touching the same.* London, 1648.

Ames, William. *De Conscientia et eius iure, vel casibus, libri quinque.* . . . Amstel., 1631. Trans. as *Conscience, with the Power and Cases thereof.* London, 1639.

Baronius, Caesar Cardinal. *Annales ecclesiastici.* Rome, 1590.

Bibliotheca Biblica. Being a Commentary upon all the books of the Old and New Testament. Gather'd out of the genuine writings of Fathers and ecclesiastical historians, and acts of Councils. To which are added introductory discourses . . . with notes and scholia, etc. [By Samuel Parker of T.C. Oxford, first five volumes only published at Oxford, 1720–35, from the 1611 version.]

Bradwardine, Thomas, Archbishop of Canterbury. *De Causa Dei contra Pelagium.* . . . London, 1618.

Calvin, Jean. *Institutio Christianae Religionis.* . . . Basileae, 1536.

Calvisius, Seth Heinrich. *Chronologia ex autoritate potissimum Sacrae Scripturae, et historicorum fide dignissimorum.* . . . Lipsiae, 1605.

Casaubon, Isaac. *De rebus sacris et ecclesiasticis exercitationes XVI.* London, 1614.

Castellio, Sebastinanus (Sébastien Châteillon). *Sebastiani Castellionis Dialogi IV. De praedestinatione. Electione. Libero arbitrio. Fide.* Goudae, 1613.

[Charles the First?]. *Eikon Basilike. The Pourtraicture of His Sacred Maiestie in his solitudes and sufferings.* London, 1648.

———. *The Papers which passed at New-Castle betwixt His Sacred Majestie and Mr. Al: Henderson: concerning the Change of Church-Government* [1646]. London, 1649.

Cole, H. (Provost of Eton). *The Holy Table, Name and Thing, more anciently . . . used . . . then that of an Altar.* [London?] 1637 [reply to Peter Heylyn].

Cosin, John (Bishop of Durham). *The Correspondence of John Cosin, D.D. Lord Bishop of Durham . . .* Edited by C. Ornsby. Durham, 1869.

Dering, Edward. *A Sparing Restraint, of many lauishe Vntruthes, which M. Doctor Harding dothe chalenge, in the first article of my Lorde of Sarisburies Replie* [containing an answer to Harding's answer to Jewel]. London, 1568.

Evelyn, John. *The Diary and Correspondence of John Evelyn,* edited by William Bray and revised by Henry Wheatley. 4 vols. Oxford, 1906.

———. *Memoirs for my Grand-Son,* edited by Sir Geoffrey Keynes. London, 1926.

Fell, John. *The Life of the Most Learned . . . and Pious Dr. H. Hammond,* London, 1661.

Fisher, Edward. *An answer to sixteen queries touching the . . . observation of Christmass, propounded by J. Hemming.* (John) Baron Somers, *A Collection of Scarce and Valuable Tracts.* Vol. IV. London, 1748.

Goodwin, John, Vicar of St. Stephen's, Coleman Street. . . . *Redemption Redeemed . . . Together with a sober . . . discussion of Election and Reprobation.* London, 1651.

Gr[antham], Vicar of. *A Coale from the Altar. Or, an answer to a Letter not long since written* [by J. Williams, Bishop of Lincoln] *to the Vicar of Gr[antham] against the placing of the Communion Table at the East end of the Chancell . . . First sent* [by Peter Heylyn] *for the satisfaction of his private friend.* London, 1636.

Bibliography

Hales, John ["the ever Memorable"]. *Golden Remains*. London, 1673.

Hammond, Henry. *Dissertationes quatuor . . . contra sententiam D. Blondelli*. London, 1651.

Heylyn, Peter. *A Coale from the Altar. Or an answer to a letter* [by J. Williams, Bishop of Lincoln] *against the placing of the Communion Table at the East end of the Chancell*. London, 1636.

Hoard, Samuel. *Gods Love to Mankind Manifested, by dis-prooving his absolute decree for their damnation*. London, 1635.

Jeanes, Henry. *A vindication of D. Twisse from the Exceptions of J. Goodwin in his Redemption redeemed*. London, 1653.

———. *A Second part of The Mixture of Scholastical Divinity* [first part pub. in 1656] *. . . Whereunto are annexed several letters of the same author, and Dr. Jeremy Taylor, concerning original sin*. Oxford, 1660.

Jewel, John (Bishop of Salisbury). *An Apology . . . in defence of the Church of England . . . newly set forth in Latine and now translated into Englishe*. London, 1562.

———. *Ioannis Iuelli . . . adversus T. Hardingum volumen alterum* [i.e., "A Replie unto M. Hardinges answeare"]. London, 1578.

Montagu, Richard. *A Gagg for the New Gospell?* etc. [against Matthew Kellison]. London, 1624.

———. *Appello Caesarem*. London, 1625.

———. *De Originibus Ecclesiasticis commentationum tomus primus*. London, 1636.

N., O. *An Apology of English Arminianisme, or a dialogue, between Jacobus Arminius . . . and Enthusiastus an English Doctour of Divinity and a great Precisian*. London, 1634.

Perkins, William. *De Praedestinationis Modo et ordine* [1598], trans. as *A Christian and plaine Treatise of the manner and order of Predestination, and of the largeness of God's Grace*. London, 1606(?).

Pocklington, John. *Altare christianum: or the Dead Vicars Plea, wherein the Vicar of Gr*[antham] *being dead, yet speaketh and pleadeth out of Antiquity, against him that hath broken down his Altar*. London, 1637.

Prynne, William. *A Quench-Coale; or, A Brief Disquisition and Inquirie in what place of the Church or Chancell the Lords-*

Table ought to be situate especially when the Sacrament is Administered. London, 1637.

Rutherford, Samuel. *A Free Disputation against pretended Liberty of Conscience, tending to resolve doubts moved by Mr. J. Goodwin, John Baptist, Dr. Jer. Taylor . . . and other authors contending for lawlesse liberty, or licentious toleration of Sects and heresies.* London, 1649.

Thomason Tracts, The. *Catalogue of the Pamphlets, Books, Newspapers and Manuscripts . . . Collected by George Thomason, 1640–61,* edited by G. K. Fortescue. 2 vols. London, 1908.

Thorndike, Herbert. *An Epilogue to the Tragedy of the Church of England . . . occasioned by the present calamity. . . .* London, 1659.

Twisse, William. *The Riches of God's Love unto the Vessels of Mercy consistent with His Absolute Hatred or Reprobation of the Vessels of Wrath; or An Answer unto a book entitled God's Love unto Mankind, Manifested by Disproving His Absolute Decree for their Damnation.* Oxford, 1653.

Ward, Samuel. *A Coal from the Altar to kindle the holy fire of zeale. In a sermon* [on Rev. 3:19]. London, 1618, 1622.

[Westminster Assembly]. *The Directory for the Publique Worship of God.* London, 1645.

Books and Articles on Jeremy Taylor since His Time

Addison, James T. "Jeremy Taylor, Preacher and Pastor." *Historical Magazine of the Protestant Episcopal Church,* XXI (1949), 148–90.

Antoine, Sister M. S. *The Rhetoric of Jeremy Taylor's Prose: Ornament of the Sunday Sermons.* Washington, D.C., 1946.

Armstrong, Martin. *Jeremy Taylor: a Selection from his Works.* Waltham St. Lawrence, 1923.

B.S. Esq., Barrister at Law. *The Beauties of Jeremy Taylor selected from all his devotional Writings and Sermons, with a Biographical Notice, and a Critical Examination of His Genius and Style.* London, 1845.

Barksdale, Clement. *A Remembrancer of Excellent Men.* London, 1670.

Barry, Alfred. "Jeremy Taylor, the English Chrysostom," in *The Classic Preachers of the English Church.* London, 1878.

Bibliography

Bentley, G. B. "Jeremy Taylor's *Ductor Dubitantium*," *Theology*, I (1947), 182–86.

Bolton, Frederick Rothwell. *The Caroline Tradition of the Church of Ireland, with particular reference to Bishop Jeremy Taylor.* London, 1958.

Bonney, Henry K. *The Life of . . . Jeremy Taylor . . . Lord Bishop of Connor, and Dromore.* London, 1815.

Brinkley, Roberta Florence. "Coleridge's Criticism of Jeremy Taylor." *Huntington Library Quarterly*, XIII (1950), 313–23.

———, ed. *Coleridge on the Seventeenth Century.* Durham, N.C., 1955.

Browne, W. J. *Jeremy Taylor.* London, 1925.

———. "Jeremy Taylor's Sermons." *TLS*, January 11, 1952, p. 25.

Brush, John. "*The Liberty of Prophesying:* A Tercentenary Essay of Appreciation." *Crozier Quarterly*, XXV (1948), 216–23.

Burgesse, Anthony. *A Treatise of Original Sin.* London, 1658.

Cattermole, Richard, ed. *The Liberty of Prophesying by Jeremy Taylor.* The Sacred Classics. London, 1834.

Coleridge, Samuel T. *See* Brinkley.

Cooper, Anthony, Earl of Shaftsbury. *Characteristics of Men and Manners.* 3 vols. London, 1711.

Cox, George W. *A Book of Family Prayer, compiled chiefly from the Devotions of Jeremy Taylor.* London, 1862.

Cropper, Margaret. *Flame Touches Flame: Six Anglican Saints of the Seventeenth Century.* London, 1958.

dePauley, W. C. "A Study in Christian Perfection," *Hermathena*, XC (1957), 3–16.

De Quincey, Thomas. *The Collected Writings of Thomas De Quincey.* Edited by David Masson. Edinburgh, 1890.

Duyckinck, George L. *The Life of Jeremy Taylor.* New York, 1860.

Elmen, Paul. "Jeremy Taylor and the Fall of Man." *Modern Language Quarterly*, XIV (1953), 139–48.

Farrar, F. W. In A. Barry's *Masters in English Theology.* London, 1877.

Gathorn-Hardy, R. *Bibliography of Jeremy Taylor*, in L. P. Smith, *Golden Grove;* enlarged in *TLS*, September 25, October 2, October 9 [G. Keynes], 1930; September 15, 1932 [important]; 20, 1947; *Library* II (1947–48), III (1948–49).

———. "Jeremy Taylor and 'Christian Consolation.'" *TLS*, April 20, 1951, p. 241.

———. "Jeremy Taylor and Halton's *Psalter of David*." *TLS*, February 18, 1953, p. 112.

George, E. *Seventeenth Century Men of Latitude*. London, 1908.

Gest, M., ed. *The House of Understanding*. Philadelphia, 1954.

Glicksman, Harry. "The Figurative Quality in Jeremy Taylor's *Holy Dying*." *Sewanee Review*, XXX (1922), 488–94.

Gosse, Sir Edmund. *Jeremy Taylor*. English Men of Letters Series. London, 1904.

Greenslade, B. D. "Jeremy Taylor in 1655." *N & Q*, CXCVI (March 17, 1951), 130.

Hazlitt, William. *Lectures Chiefly on the Dramatic Literature of the Age of Elizabeth*. London, 1820.

Heltzel, Virgil, ed. "Richard Earl of Carbery's Advice to His Son." *Huntington Library Bulletin*, no. 11 (1937), pp. 59–105.

Herndon, S. "Jeremy Taylor's Use of the Bible." Ph.D. dissertation, New York University, 1949.

Hoopes, Robert. "Voluntarism in Jeremy Taylor and the Platonic Tradition." *Huntington Library Quarterly*, XIII (1950), 341–54.

Hughes, H. Trevor. *The Piety of Jeremy Taylor*. London, 1960.

Hughes, T. S. *The Works of Jeremy Taylor, D.D.* 5 vols. London, 1831.

["J.W."] *The Clergyman's Companion in Visiting the Sick . . . extracted Chiefly from Bishop Taylor*. London, 1773. Added to and reissued by William Paley of Carlisle, London, 1805.

Jackson, Robert S. "The Meditative Life of Christ: A Study of the Background and Structure of Jeremy Taylor's *The Great Exemplar*." Ph.D. dissertation, University of Michigan, 1959.

Janelle, Pierre. "English Devotional Literature in the 16th and 17th Centuries." *English Studies Today*, II (1959), 159–71.

Jeremy Taylor: Brief Passages from his Writings. London, 1882.

Kepler, Thomas, ed. *The Rule and Exercise of Holy Living*. Cleveland, Ohio, 1952.

King, James Roy. "Certain Aspects of Jeremy Taylor's Prose Style." *English Studies*, XXXVII (1956), 197–210.

———. *Studies in Six Seventeenth Century Writers*. Athens, Ohio, 1966.

Lamb, Charles. *The Letters of Charles Lamb*, edited by George Woodcock. London, 1950.

Bibliography

Lawler, H. J. "Two Letters of Jeremy Taylor." *Church of Ireland Gazette*, June 14, 1901.

May, E. H. *A Dissertation of the Life, Theology, and Times of Dr. Jeremy Taylor.* London, 1892.

Merriman, D. *Jeremy Taylor and English Liberty in the English Church.* Worcester, Mass., 1907.

Nicolson, Marjorie Hope. "New Material on Jeremy Taylor." *Philological Quarterly*, VIII (1920), 321–34.

Nossen, Robert. "Jeremy Taylor: 17th Century Theologian." *Anglican Theological Review*, XLII (1960), 28–39.

*Peterson, Raymond A., Jr. "The Theology of Jeremy Taylor: An Investigation of the Temper of Caroline Anglicanism." *Dissertation Abstracts*, XXI (1961). Ph.D. dissertation, Union Theological Seminary.

Powicke, Frank J. "Jeremy Taylor and his Doctrine of Toleration." *Constructive Quarterly*, September, 1915, pp. 657–77.

Praz, Mario. "Baroque in England." *Modern Philology*, LXI (1963), 169–79.

———. *Studies in 17th Century Imagery*, 2d ed. Rome, 1964.

Ross Williamson, Hugh. *Jeremy Taylor.* A Pegasus Biography. London, 1952.

Smith, L. P., ed. *The Golden Grove: Selected Passages from the Sermons and Writings of Jeremy Taylor, with a Bibliography . . . by Robert Gathorne-Hardy.* Oxford, 1930.

Stedmond, J. M. "English Prose of the Seventeenth Century." *Dalhousie Review*, XXX (1951) 269–78.

Steffan, T. Guy. "Jeremy Taylor's Criticism of Abstract Speculation." *University of Texas Studies in English*, XX (1940), 96–108.

Stephens, Sir James. *Horae Sabbaticae.* London, 1892.

Stranks, C. J. "Jeremy Taylor", *Church Quarterly Review*, CXXXI (1940), 31–63.

———. *The Life and Writings of Jeremy Taylor.* London, 1952.

Wheeldon, John. *The Life of Bp. Taylor.* London, 1789.

White, Newport. *Four Good Men.* Dublin, 1927.

Willmott, Rev. R. A. *Bishop Jeremy Taylor, His Predecessors, Contemporaries, and Successors.* London, 1847.

Wilson, F. P. *Seventeenth Century Prose: Five Lectures.* Berkeley, Calif., 1960.

Wood, Thomas. *English Casuistical Divinity during the Seventeenth*

Century with Special Reference to Jeremy Taylor. London, 1952.

Worley, George. *Jeremy Taylor: A Sketch of His Life and Times, with a Popular Exposition of His Works.* London, 1904.

General Works on the Religious, Political, and Literary Milieu

Acontius. *Satan's Strategems.* Translated by Walter T. Curtis. San Francisco, 1940.

Adams, W. H. Davenport. *Great English Churchmen.* London, 1879.

Arminius. *The Writings of Arminius.* Vols. I and II translated by James Nichols (London, 1925–28); Vol. III translated by W. R. Bagnall. Grand Rapids, Mich., 1956.

Addleshaw, G. W. O. *The High Church Tradition: A Study in the Liturgical Thought of the Seventeenth Century.* London, 1941.

Arnold, Matthew. *Lectures and Essays in Criticism.* Edited by R. H. Super. Ann Arbor, Mich., 1962.

Bainton, Roland H. "Sebastian Castellio and the Toleration Controversy of the Sixteenth Century." *Persecution and Liberty: Essays in Honor of George Lincoln Burr.* New York, 1931.

Baker, Herschel. *The Wars of Truth: Studies in the Decay of Christian Humanism in the Earlier Seventeenth Century,* Cambridge, Mass., 1952.

Beckett, Matthew. *Sir George Rawdon. A Sketch of his Life and Times.* Belfast, 1935.

Beum, Robert. "The Scientific Affinities of English Baroque Prose." *English Miscellany,* XIII (1962), 59–80.

Bush, Douglas. *English Literature of the Earlier Seventeenth Century, 1600–1660.* 2nd ed. Oxford, 1962.

Carlyle, Thomas. *Cromwell's Letters and Speeches.* Edited by S. C. Lomas. London, 1904.

Cassirer, Ernest. *The Platonic Renaissance in England.* Translated by James P. Pettegrove. Edinburgh, 1953.

Chittick, Roger Dale. "The Augustinian Tradition in 17th Century English Prose." *Dissertation Abstracts* XVII (1957). Ph.D. dissertation, Leland Stanford University.

Clarendon, Edward Hyde, Earl of. *The History of the Rebellion and Civil Wars in England.* 2 vols. Oxford, 1843.

Bibliography

Clarke, W. K. L., and C. Harris, *Liturgy and Worship*. New York, 1932.

Colie, Rosalie L. *Light and Enlightenment: A Study of the Cambridge Platonists and the Dutch Arminians*. Cambridge, 1957.

Collins, W. E. *Typical English Churchmen*. London, 1902.

Conklin, George N. *Biblical Criticism and Heresy in Milton*. New York, 1949.

Cope, Jackson I. "Seventeenth Century Quaker Style." *PMLA*, LXXI (1956), 725–54.

Costello, William T. *The Scholastic Curriculum at Early 17th Century Cambridge*. Cambridge, Mass., 1958.

Davidson, Anne Elizabeth. "Innocence Regained: 17th Century Reinterpretations of the Fall of Man." *Dissertation Abstracts* XVII (1956). Ph.D. dissertation, Columbia University.

Davies, Godfrey. "Arminian vs. Puritan in England, c. 1620–1650." *Huntington Library Bulletin*, no. 5 (1934), 157–79.

———. "Charles II in 1660." *Huntington Library Quarterly*, XIX (1956), 245–75.

———. *The Restoration of Charles II*. San Marino, Calif., 1955.

Des Maiseaux. *Life of Chillingworth*. London, 1725.

Dictionnaire d'histoire et de géographie ecclésiastique. Paris, 1912.

Ditchfield, P. H. *The Church in the Netherlands*. London, 1892.

Dowden, Edward. *Puritan and Anglican*. London, 1900.

Dugmore, C. W. *Eucharistic Doctrine in England from Hooker to Waterland*. London, 1942.

Elson, James H. *John Hales of Eton*. New York, 1948.

Emerson, Ralph Waldo. *English Traits*. Boston, 1866.

Freund, M. *Die Idee der Toleranz im England der grossen Revolution*. Halle, 1927.

Gardiner, Samuel R. *History of the Great Civil War, 1642–1649*. London, 1886–91.

Giran, Etienne. *Sébastien Castellion et la réforme calviniste*. Haarlem and Paris, 1914.

Hallam, A. D. "The Study of Hebrew in 17th Century England and its Effects on English Literature." *AUMLA Proceedings* [1], pp. 180–81.

Hamilton, K. G. *The Two Harmonies of Poetry and Prose in the 17th Century*. Oxford, 1963.

Harrison, A. H. W. *The Beginnings of Arminianism to the Synod of Dort*. London, 1926.

Hastings, James, ed. *Encyclopedia of Religion and Ethics.* Edinburgh, 1908–26.

Hearnshaw, F. J. C. *The Social and Political Ideas of Some Great Thinkers of the Sixteenth and Seventeenth Centuries.* New York, 1949.

Hill, John Edward Christopher. "The Diary of John Evelyn." *History,* XLII (1957), 12–18.

———. *Society and Puritanism in Pre-Revolutionary England.* New York, 1964.

Hilton, Walter. *The Ladder of Perfection.* Translated by Leo Sherley-Price. Harmondsworth, 1957.

Howell, Wilbur S. *Logic and Rhetoric in England, 1500–1700.* Princeton, N.J., 1956.

Hunt, John. *Religious Thought in England from the Reformation to the end of the Last Century.* London, 1870–73.

Huntley, Frank L. "Heads for an Essay on the 17th Century Anglican Funeral Sermon in England." *Anglican Theological Review,* XXXVIII (1956), 226–34.

———. *Sir Thomas Browne: A Biographical and Critical Study.* Ann Arbor, Mich., 1962.

Huttar, Charles A. "English Metrical Paraphrases of the Psalms, 1500–1640." *Dissertation Abstracts* XVI (1956), 631–32. Ph.D. dissertation, Northwestern University.

Jones, Richard F. "The Rhetoric of Science in England in the mid-17th Century." *Restoration and Eighteenth Century Literature,* 1963, pp. 5–24.

Jordan, Wilbur K. *The Development of Religious Toleration in England.* Cambridge, Mass., 1938.

Kirk, The Right Reverend K. E., ed. *The Epistle to the Romans.* The Clarendon Bible Series. Oxford, 1937, 1947, 1950, 1953.

Loane, Marcus L. *Makers of Religious Freedom in the Seventeenth Century: Henderson, Rutherford, Bunyan, Baxter.* Grand Rapids, Mich., 1961.

Lyon, Thomas. *The Theory of Religious Liberty in England, 1603–1639.* Cambridge, 1937.

Mackinnon, Edward. "Motion, Mechanics, and Theology." *Thought,* XXXVI (1961), 344–70.

* Macklem, Michael. *The Anatomy of the World: Relations between Natural and Moral Law from Donne to Pope.* Minneapolis, Minn., 1957.

Bibliography

Matthews, A. G., ed. *Walker Revised, being a revision of John Walker's Sufferings of the Clergy during the Grand Rebellion, 1642–1660.* Oxford, 1948.

McAdoo, H. R. *The Structure of Caroline Moral Theology.* London, 1949.

Miller, Perry. *The New England Mind.* Cambridge, Mass., 1954.

Milosh, Joseph E. *The Scale of Perfection* [by Walter Hilton] *and the English Mystical Tradition.* Madison, Wis., 1966.

Mitchell, W. F. *English Pulpit Oratory from Andrewes to Tillotson.* London, 1932.

More, P. E., and F. L. Cross, eds. *Anglicanism: The Thought and Practice of the Church of England, illustrated from the Religious Literature of the Seventeenth Century.* Milwaukee, Wis., 1935.

New Catholic Encyclopedia, The. New York, 1967.

Nichols, James. *Calvinism and Arminianism Compared.* 2 vols. London, 1824.

Nicolson, Marjorie Hope, ed. *The Conway Letters.* New Haven, Conn., 1930.

Nobbs, Douglas. *Theocracy and Toleration: A Study of the Disputes in Dutch Calvinism from 1600 to 1650.* Cambridge, 1938.

Nygren, Bishop Anders. *A Commentary on Romans.* Translated by C. C. Rasmussen. Philadelphia, 1949.

Parker, William R. *Milton: A Biography.* 2 vols. Oxford, 1968.

Parsons, Roger L. "Renaissance and Baroque: Multiple Unity and Unified Unity in the Treatment of Verse, Ornament, and Structure." *Dissertation Abstracts* XIX (1958). Ph.D dissertation, University of Wisconsin.

Patrides, C. A. "A Note on Renaissance Plagiarism." *N & Q,* n.s. III (1958), 438–39.

Plato. *The Dialogues of Plato.* Translated by Benjamin Jowett. 2 vols. New York, 1939.

Predestination, Collection of Tracts Concerning. London, 1719.

Ragsdale, J. Donald. "Invention in English 'Stylistic' Rhetorics, 1600–1800." *QJS,* LI (1965), 164–67.

Richards, Thomas. *Religious Developments in Wales, 1654–1662.* London, 1923.

Ryan, Clarence J. "Theories of Church-State Relationships in Seventeenth Century England." *Historical Bulletin,* XXVII (1949), 29–30, 36–41.

Salmon, Vivian. "Early Seventeenth Century Punctuation as a Guide to Sentence Structure." *Review of English Studies*, XII (1961), 347–60.

Shaw, William A. *A History of the English Church During the Civil Wars and Under the Commonwealth, 1640–1660.* London, 1900.

Smith, Logan Pearsall, ed. *Donne's Sermons: Selected Passages.* Oxford, 1919.

Smyth, Charles Hugh Egerton. *The Art of Preaching.* London, 1940.

Somerset, The Victoria History of the County of. London, 1906.

Stranks, Charles James. *Anglican Devotion. . . .* London, 1961.

Summers, Joseph H. *George Herbert: His Religion and Art.* London, 1954.

Sutherland, James R., and Ian Watt. *Restoration and Augustan Prose.* Los Angeles, Calif., 1956.

Swardson, Harold R. *Poetry and the Fountain of Light: Observations on the Conflict between Christian and Classical Tradition in 17th Century Poetry.* Columbia, Mo., 1961.

Sykes, Norman. *Old Priest and New Presbyter. . . .* Cambridge, 1956.

———. *The Church of England and Non-Episcopal Churches in the Sixteenth and Seventeenth Centuries.* London, 1949.

Tennant, Frederick R. *The Concept of Sin.* Cambridge, 1912.

Throckmorton, Bruce H., Jr. *Romans for the Layman.* Philadelphia, 1961.

Tulloch, John. *Rational Theology and Christian Philosophy in England in the Seventeenth Century.* London, 1872.

Tuve, Rosemund. *Elizabethan and Metaphysical Imagery.* Chicago, 1961.

Usher, Roland G. *The Reconstruction of the English Church.* New York, 1910.

Walker, Daniel P. *The Decline of Hell: Seventeenth Century Discussions of Eternal Torment.* London, 1964.

Warren, Austin. *Richard Crashaw: A Study in Baroque Sensibility.* Baton Rouge, La., 1939.

Wedgwood, C. V. *The King's Peace, 1637–1641.* London, 1955.

———. *Seventeenth-Century English Literature.* Oxford, 1961.

Westfall, Richard S. *Science and Religion in 17th Century England.* New Haven, Conn., 1958.

Bibliography

Whitelock, Sir Bulstrode. *Memorials of the English Affairs.* . . . London, 1682.

Wiley, Margaret L. *The Subtle Knot: Creative Scepticism in Seventeenth Century England.* London, 1952.

Williams, Franklin B., Jr. "The Laudian Imprimatur." *Library,* XV (1960), 96–104.

Williams, Norman P. *The Ideas of the Fall and Original Sin.* London, 1927.

Williamson, George. *Seventeenth Century Contexts.* London, 1960.

Wood, Thomas. "The Seventeenth Century English Casuists on Betting and Gambling." *Church Quarterly Review,* CXLIX (1951), 159–74.

Wyndham, Henry P. *A Gentleman's Tour through Monmouthshire and Wales.* London, 1781.

Zweig, Stefan. *Ein Gewissen gegen die Gewalt. Castellio gegen Calvin.* Berlin, 1951.

Index

Index

Hammond, the Rev. Henry, 3, 64, 99
Hastings, James, 109
Hatton, Sir Christopher, 9, 10, 15, 19, 32, 35–6, 50, 51
Heber, Bp. Reginald, vii, 7, 9, 24, 31, 51, 59, 61, 102, 105, 108
Heltzel, Virgil, 107
Henderson, the Rev. Alexander, 3, 26, 107
Henry the Eighth, 8, 26
Herbert, George, 22, 55, 107
Hermengilda, St., 97
Heylin, the Rev. Peter, 23, 24
Hilton, Walter, 15, 106
Histriomastix, 23
Hoard, the Rev. Samuel, 75
Hooker, Richard, 14, 94, 102
Howard, Sir Robert, 112
Huxley, Aldous, 47
Hyde, Edward First Earl of Clarendon, 33, 107

Independents, 39, 51, 54, 86
Isaiah, 58

Jackson, Dean Thomas, 75
James, St., 17
Jeanes, the Rev. Henry, 75, 77, 93, 94
Jerome, St., 17, 85
Jerusalem, 17
Jesuits, 24, 52, 69, 70, 84, 92
Jewel, Bp. John, 17, 26
John the Baptist, 58
Jones, the Rev. Gordon M., Jr., ix
Jordan, W. K., viii, 108
Julian, 92
Junius, Franz, Sr., 72
Jupiter, 85
Justin, St. (Martyr), 85
Juxon, Archbp. William, 24

Kant, Emanuel, 112
Kellison, Matthew, 3
Kemey, Sir Nicholas, 62
Keynes, Sir Geoffrey, 108
Kirk, Bp. K. E., 102

Lamb, Charles, ii, 111

Laud, Archbp. William, vii, 3, 11, 13, 17, 24, 26, 54, 105, 106
Laugharne, General Rowland, 23–3
Lazarus, 40
le Franc, Mons. J., 67
Leslie, Henry, 98
Linus, St., 17
Lichfield, Leonard (printer), 13
Lisnagarvey (Lisburn), 95, 98
Loane, Marcus L., 107
Lombard, Peter, 69
Lombart, Pierre (engraver), 59
Loudun, the devils of, 47
Lucian, 47
Lutheran, 70, 98

MacKelvey, Frank, 98
Mark, St., 17
Marshall, Will (engraver), 34
Marten, Harry (regicide), 62
Matthews, Le., 99
Mary and Martha, 15, 40, 58
Maximus (tyrant), 49
McAdoo, H. R., 51, 105
Milosh, Joseph E., 106
Milton, John, viii, 7, 14, 33, 35, 37, 54, 73, 79, 82, 86, 100, 101, 102
Minerva, 85
Molucca Islands, 88
Montague, Bp. Richard, 3, 18
Montaigne, 2, 44
More, Henry, 98
More, St. Thomas, 14
Morgan, Col. Thomas, 62
Moses, 53, 80–1

Newman, John Henry Cardinal, 1, 4, 15
New Model Army, 45
Nicene Council, 41
Nicene Creed, 53
Nicolson, Marjorie, 97
Norris, John, 14
Nygren, Bp. Anders, 102

Occam, 69
Origen, 68
Ormond, Duke of, 96
Overal, Bp. John, 3

Index

DATE DUE